W9-CIN-094

NEW DIRECTIONS FOR HIGHER EDUCATION

Martin Kramer
EDITOR-IN-CHIEF

The Experience of Being in Graduate School: An Exploration

Melissa S. Anderson
University of Minnesota

EDITOR

Number 101, Spring 1998

JOSSEY-BASS PUBLISHERS
San Francisco

THE EXPERIENCE OF BEING IN GRADUATE
SCHOOL: AN EXPLORATION
Melissa S. Anderson (ed.)
New Directions for Higher Education, no. 101
Volume XXVI, Number 1
Martin Kramer, Editor-in-Chief

Microfilm copies of issues and articles are available in 16mm and 35mm,
as well as microfiche in 105mm, through University Microfilms Inc., 300
North Zeeb Road, Ann Arbor, Michigan 48106-1346.

ISSN 0271-0560   ISBN 0-7879-4247-2

NEW DIRECTIONS FOR HIGHER EDUCATION is part of The Jossey-Bass
Higher and Adult Education Series and is published quarterly by Jossey-
Bass Inc., Publishers, 350 Sansome Street, San Francisco, California
94104-1342. Periodicals postage paid at San Francisco, California, and at
additional mailing offices. POSTMASTER: Send address changes to New
Directions for Higher Education, Jossey-Bass Inc., Publishers, 350 Sansome Street, San Francisco, California 94104-1342.

SUBSCRIPTIONS cost $54.00 for individuals and $90.00 for institutions,
agencies, and libraries.

EDITORIAL CORRESPONDENCE should be sent to the Editor-in-Chief, Martin
Kramer, 2807 Shasta Road, Berkeley, California 94708-2011.

Cover photograph and random dot by Richard Blair/Color & Light © 1990.

Jossey-Bass Web address: www.josseybass.com

Printed in the United States of America on acid-free recycled paper con-
taining 100 percent recovered waste paper, of which at least 20 percent is
postconsumer waste.

CONTENTS

Editor's Notes

In the vast expanse of postsecondary education, graduate education is a relatively small sector. There is much at stake, however, in the graduate enterprise. Here students are prepared to become leaders, professionals, researchers, and scholars who will be responsible for the advancement of our knowledge and well-being. Graduate faculties, specialized instruction, research facilities, libraries, and other resources are all expensive. Not surprisingly, most of what is written about graduate education has to do with federal and other investments, supply and demand in academic and professional labor markets, and programs of advanced instruction and research.

But what of the students themselves? What do they go through in graduate school? What is the graduate experience like? Here, too, there is much at stake. Graduate study often spans many years of challenges and intense work. Many students, however, have little idea of what graduate school entails and begin graduate programs with no real sense of what they will be expected to do. Even students with exemplary academic records and high aspirations can be deflected from the graduate degree course by bad experiences in graduate school. Some leave. Some drag out their graduate work for years beyond the norm. Some drift away in perpetual ABD (all but dissertation) status, without ever fully resolving either to complete the degree or to quit. Some receive good preparation for certain aspects of their prospective career, such as research, but not others, such as teaching. Some are prepared narrowly for positions that they have very little likelihood of ever attaining due to job market conditions. Students may even learn things in their graduate years that contribute in the long run to dysfunction or at least suboptimality in the academy, such as extreme competition and self-interest.

This volume addresses the graduate experience from the standpoint of students themselves. All of the authors of these chapters were invited to contribute because they are involved in research or programs directly related to the experiences of graduate students; they all wrote about student experiences from firsthand data of one kind or another. From a variety of perspectives and across many fields of study, these chapters present what students themselves have reported about their experiences through interviews, surveys, ongoing discussions, and autobiographies.[1]

In Chapter One, Judith P. Swazey and I provide an overview of the Ph.D. experience, based on a national survey of doctoral students. Chapter Two, by Steven Weiland, takes a long-term view of graduate education through autobiographical accounts of graduate study. Beth A. Fischer and Michael J.

I wish to extend my sincere appreciation to Janet M. Holdsworth for her research assistance and to Dee Wasilak for her secretarial assistance on this volume.

Zigmond, in Chapter Three, describe what doctoral students need to know, based on the authors' experiences with the University of Pittsburgh's Survival Skills and Ethics Program.

The next two chapters describe some of the changes graduate students go through during the course of a graduate program. Marcia B. Baxter Magolda, in Chapter Four, uses an epistemological lens to examine students' intellectual development during graduate school. In Chapter Five, Chris M. Golde analyzes students' experiences in graduate programs to see what leads some students to leave programs at an early stage.

Chapter Six, by Clifton F. Conrad, Katherine M. Duren, and Jennifer Grant Haworth, discusses students' experiences in master's degree programs. Chapter Seven, by Jerry G. Gaff and Anne S. Pruitt-Logan, and Chapter Eight, by Peg Boyle and Robert Boice, present recommendations for improving students' preparation for faculty careers and their enculturation into the department and the profession. Finally, Jules B. LaPidus, from his standpoint as president of the Council of Graduate Schools, presents an overview in Chapter Nine of the changing nature of graduate education and suggests how graduate education can address issues presented in the previous chapters.

If students knew more about the graduate experience beforehand, perhaps some of them would avoid what would be, for them, the costly mistake of entering graduate school. Those who begin graduate programs would have a better sense of what their work and life would be like. With a broader view of graduate education, graduate students would understand better whether their experiences were typical or rare, expected or inappropriate, to be rejected or to be endured.

If faculty and administrators knew more about graduate school experiences, beyond their own, they might be more aware of how those experiences could be improved or enhanced. With substantial investments in research, graduate instruction and advising, facilities, and administration, universities need to learn how to make the best use of their graduate-education capacity. In particular, they need to avoid the enormous waste of effort and resources that accompanies the loss of a promising graduate student.

Melissa S. Anderson
Editor

Note

1. This volume includes many direct quotations from students themselves; the authors and editors have gone to great lengths to ensure that none of the texts or quotations identifies individual students.

MELISSA S. ANDERSON is associate professor of higher education at the University of Minnesota. Her current research includes the Academic Life Project (an NSF-funded longitudinal study of the doctoral experience), as well as continuing work on academic-industry relationships and faculty demography in academic departments.

A national survey of doctoral students sought students' reflections on their graduate experiences, their faculty, their department, their academic work, and their prospective careers.

Reflections on the Graduate Student Experience: An Overview

Melissa S. Anderson, Judith P. Swazey

In studying the doctoral experience, there is no substitute for on-site, interview, or observation-based data collection. Surveys, however, offer an opportunity to collect information on a broad scale to examine patterns of experience and particularly to investigate the prevalence of certain experiences that people normally associate with graduate school largely because of the stories they hear. The doctoral-student surveys of the Acadia Institute's Project on Professional Values and Ethical Issues in the Graduate Education of Scientists and Engineers[1] included a range of questions about students' experiences in their graduate program. They addressed students' reasons for going to graduate school, their graduate work and evaluation of that work, the organizational climate of their graduate department, their affective responses to the demands of graduate study, and students' assessments of the graduate experience and their prospective career. These questions are the basis for this analysis of the doctoral experience.

We sent the surveys to 2,000 doctoral students in the fall of 1989. We selected the students randomly from ninety-nine departments in chemistry, civil engineering, microbiology, and sociology at major research universities in the United States. The response rate was 72 percent. Further details about the survey and related research results appear in previous Acadia Graduate Education Project publications. These include articles on academic misconduct (Anderson, 1996b; Anderson, Louis, and Earle, 1994; Louis, Anderson, and Rosenberg, 1995; Swazey, Anderson, and Louis, 1993), mentoring (Anderson and Oju, in press; Swazey and Anderson, 1996), collaboration in graduate programs (Anderson, 1996a), and norms of academic research (Anderson and Louis, 1994).

New Directions for Higher Education, no. 101, Spring 1998 © Jossey-Bass Publishers

Why Do Students Go to Graduate School?

We asked students how important certain factors were to their decision to attend graduate school. The survey items, ranked here by frequency of "very important" responses, appear in Table 1.1. Not surprisingly, over three-quarters of our respondents said that a desire for knowledge in the field of study was very important. About two-thirds indicated that wanting to do research was a very important factor, whereas very few said that research was unimportant to their decision. A substantial 40 percent noted that their desire to teach at the college or university level was a very important part of their reason for going to graduate school, but fully 29 percent said that wanting to teach was not very or not at all important. In chemistry and microbiology, the responses to the teaching item were split nearly evenly among "very," "somewhat," and "not very/not at all" important, but in sociology just over half said that wanting to teach was a very important factor. Such a difference probably reflects varying opportunities for scientists and social scientists to pursue research or teaching careers.

Wanting to help others clearly won out over advancement in employment or a high-paying job as a factor in the decision to attend graduate school. Fewer than half of our respondents said that the lifestyle of a scientist[2] or "the high regard in which scientists are held" had anything to do with their going to graduate school. Interestingly, 23 percent admitted that not being able to think of anything better to do had at least some effect on their decision to begin doctoral study.

What Do Doctoral Students Think of Their Academic Work?

Once students get into graduate school, their academic work is dominated by three activities: taking courses, doing research for the dissertation or other projects, and, in most departments, completing preliminary or comprehensive examinations or papers. Many of our respondents, ranging from a 25 percent in sociology to 40 percent in chemistry and microbiology, said that they had little choice as to which courses they could take because of the number of required courses. Overall, about half said that their faculty really cared about teaching, except in civil engineering, for which that figure reached 70 percent. As Table 1.2 shows, 65 percent thought that their coursework laid a good foundation for doing independent work, and nearly that many thought that their faculty had exposed them to a wide variety of useful research experiences.

In graduate school, students encounter what for many is a new aspect of academic work: independent research. Nearly 90 percent of our respondents agreed that graduate students were encouraged to be self-directed. Our findings, however, counter the common image of a solitary doctoral student toiling alone on a dissertation. Of the science and engineering students surveyed, between 55 and 60 percent said that most students did their dissertation

Table 1.1. Reasons for Going to Graduate School

	Very	Somewhat	Not Very or Not at All
How important were the following factors in your decision to go to graduate school?			
Desire for knowledge in this field	78 percent	21 percent	2 percent
Desire to do research in this field	66	28	6
Desire to teach in higher education	40	31	29
Desire to benefit others through this work	37	45	18
Desire to advance in my current employment	23	22	56
Desire for a job that pays well	16	37	48
The lifestyle of a scientist	15	29	56
The high regard in which scientists are held	13	34	53
Desire to change careers	13	17	71
Couldn't think of anything better to do	6	17	77

Note: Percentages may not add to 100 due to rounding.

Source: Acadia Institute Project on Professional Values and Ethical Issues in the Graduate Education of Scientists and Engineers.

Table 1.2. Graduate Work and Evaluation

	Strongly Agree	Agree	Disagree	Strongly Disagree
My coursework has laid a good foundation for doing independent work.	15 percent	50 percent	28 percent	8 percent
The faculty have exposed me to a wide variety of useful research experiences.	11	52	27	9
Graduate students are encouraged to be self-directed.	28	60	11	1
Students have little contact with each other.	2	18	48	32
Students who go through the program together learn more from each other than from faculty.	15	40	40	5
Research assistants are carefully supervised by faculty.	11	61	22	6
Teaching assistants are carefully supervised by faculty.	3	37	41	19
My graduate assistant obligations are delaying my progress.	9	26	49	17
Faculty members are explicit in their expectations of students.	4	45	38	13
Evaluation of students successfully "weeds out" weak doctoral students.	4	44	40	13

	Always or Usually	Sometimes	Rarely or Never
When your work is evaluated, how often do you find the evaluation:			
Promptly provided	57 percent	31 percent	12 percent
Detailed	46	35	19
Constructive	74	21	5
Humiliating	6	22	72

Note: Percentages may not add to 100 due to rounding.

Source: Acadia Institute Project on Professional Values and Ethical Issues in the Graduate Education of Scientists and Engineers.

research as part of a larger, collaborative project (but only 17 percent of the sociology students gave this response). Presumably reflecting both their collaborative work patterns and informal interactions, 80 percent disagreed that the statement "Students have little contact with each other" characterized their department. Such contact can be extremely important to graduate students. About half of our respondents said that the students in their program learned more from each other than from the faculty. (Chemistry students were the exception here, of which only about a third gave this response.)

Academic work is not the only task of graduate school for most students. Most are employed through at least part of their graduate work. Of our respondents, two-thirds had held research assistantships and nearly as many had been teaching assistants. About 15 percent had held other kinds of positions at their own universities, and 20 percent had worked off-campus during their graduate study. To get some sense of the quality of the experience as training for future work, we asked how well graduate assistants were supervised. Seventy-two percent of our respondents agreed that research assistants were carefully supervised by faculty, but only 40 percent made the same assessment about teaching assistants. Interestingly, students who had held a research or teaching assistantship were less likely to agree that assistants in the same category were well supervised. Over one-third said that their graduate assistant obligations delayed their progress. Though such delays could be cause for concern, they might in some cases reflect an accumulation of experience that could serve students well on completion of the Ph.D.

Evaluation is a critical part of the graduate experience because of the certifying role of the graduate degree (Baird, 1990). Students appeared unconvinced that the evaluation role was well articulated or effective: Only about half agreed—very few strongly—that faculty members were explicit in their expectations of students and that evaluation was successful in "weeding out" the weak students. As to their own experiences of evaluation, most students agreed that it was generally prompt, detailed, and constructive, but 28 percent said that it was at least sometimes humiliating.

How Do Doctoral Students View the Climate of Their Department?

The Acadia Graduate Education Project investigated not only students' own experiences in graduate school but also their views of the climate of their department (see Table 1.3). Organizational climate has proved to be a very important factor in understanding academic misconduct and other aspects of research and graduate education related to values and ethics (Anderson, 1996b; Anderson, Louis, and Earle, 1994). Here we examine individual items from the scales used in previous publications to investigate students' experiences with and within their department. We introduced these items on the survey as follows: "Please indicate the extent to which, in your experience, each statement applies to your department/program."

The first seven items in Table 1.3 reflect aspects of a community-oriented organizational climate. Over two-thirds of our respondents said that students and faculty in their department cared about each other and that students were treated with respect. Even more (around 90 percent) said that their graduate faculty were accessible to students and that students collaborated with faculty on publications. There were, however, considerable disciplinary differences in responses to these items. In each case, students in sociology were least likely to say that the given item applied to their department "to a great extent"; that is, sociology students were least likely to find their department characterized by the kind of community that these items reflect. The difference was most extreme in the case of collaboration: 70 percent of chemistry students but only 15 percent of sociology students indicated that student-faculty collaboration

Table 1.3. Climates of Graduate Programs

	Great Extent	Some Extent	Very Little or Not at All
Community:			
Students and faculty care about each other.	13 percent	61 percent	26 percent
Graduate students are treated with respect.	15	55	30
Faculty are accessible to graduate students.	41	50	9
Students and faculty collaborate on publications.	51	37	12
Faculty make sure that students feel like members of the department.	17	48	34
Graduate students are given an active role in departmental decisions that affect them.	5	32	63
There is a sense of solidarity among the students who enter the program at the same time.	29	49	22
Competition:			
People put their own interests first.	39	53	8
Faculty seem more concerned with furthering their own career than with the well-being of the department as a whole.	25	46	29
People have to compete for departmental resources.	28	44	29
Students have to compete for faculty time and attention.	13	43	44
A few students get most of the attention and resources.	13	37	50
Faculty are willing to bend the rules for some students but not for others.	12	37	52

Note: Percentages may not add to 100 due to rounding.

Source: Acadia Institute Project on Professional Values and Ethical Issues in the Graduate Education of Scientists and Engineers.

characterized their department to a great extent. The two remaining community items represent graduate-student participation in decision making, which roughly a third of our respondents thought characterized their department, and solidarity among graduate students who entered the program together, which nearly 80 percent observed at least to some extent in their department.

The remaining climate-related items in Table 1.3 center on competitive aspects of academic departments. An astounding 92 percent of our respondents said that in their department people put their own interests first. Over 70 percent said that faculty were more concerned with their career than with the good of the department and that people in their department had to compete for resources. On this last item, disciplinary differences ranged from 15 percent in chemistry to 49 percent of respondents in sociology, who said that such competition characterized their department to a great extent. Students also experienced considerable competition for attention: Roughly half said that in their department students had to compete for faculty time and attention, that a few students got most of the attention and resources, and that faculty members of their department would bend the rules for some but not all.

Clearly, the community that some students find in their department is tempered by considerable competition. In contrast to the community-climate items, every one of the competitive-climate items was most likely to be considered representative of sociology departments. We cannot know, of course, whether the sociology students see less evidence of community and more of competition because their own field of study makes them more attuned to social dimensions of organizations, because they have higher expectations about social interaction, or because their departments are genuinely less oriented to community and more to competition.

How Does the Doctoral Experience Affect Students?

One of the patterns we were particularly interested in exploring through the surveys was the prevalence of distress among graduate students. Complaints and stories of woe are part of the lore of graduate school. We chose role conflicts, faculty demands, and divestiture as aspects of the graduate experience that might reveal associated stress (see Table 1.4).

We found that substantial percentages of our respondents were always or usually bothered by role conflict: About a quarter thought they could not satisfy conflicting demands of various people, over a third thought that the amount of work they had to do interfered with how well they did it, over 40 percent felt that their work interfered with their personal life, and over a third found evaluating their own progress difficult. Given that these percentages all represent people who reported that they were bothered nearly all the time by these concerns, the common image of downtrodden doctoral students appears upheld. It is encouraging, however, that for each item a quarter or more of our students said that they were rarely or never concerned by the given issue.

Table 1.4. Student Responses to Graduate School

	Always or Usually	Sometimes	Rarely or Never
Here is a list of things that bother some graduate students. How often do they bother you?			
Thinking that I can't satisfy the conflicting demands of various people	24 percent	39 percent	37 percent
Thinking that the amount of work I have to do interferes with how well it gets done	36	40	25
Feeling that my work interferes with my personal life	42	33	25
Finding it difficult to evaluate my own progress	37	38	25

	Strongly Agree	Agree	Disagree	Strongly Disagree
Faculty expect my responsibilities as a student to come before all other responsibilities.	19 percent	44 percent	31 percent	6 percent
I often feel exploited by faculty.	6	21	48	25
Graduate school has positively reinforced my prior values, self-image, and way of thinking about the world.	10	42	30	18
Graduate school is changing me in ways I do not like.	9	23	47	22

Note: Percentages may not add to 100 due to rounding.

Source: Acadia Institute Project on Professional Values and Ethical Issues in the Graduate Education of Scientists and Engineers.

Faculty demands and expectations are, of course, a likely source of these concerns. Sixty-three percent of respondents agreed that faculty in their department expected their responsibilities as students to come before all their other responsibilities. Of even greater concern, however, is the 27 percent of our respondents who reported that they often felt exploited by faculty. Exploitation is a far different matter than high expectations. If students feel overworked because they and faculty hold different views of appropriate workloads, for example, the problem could be addressed, if not solved altogether, through more direct communication or negotiation. If, however, graduate students actually experience high levels of exploitation, considerable restructuring of tasks, responsibilities, and expectations is in order.

Even more telling, perhaps, is the extent to which graduate school as a socialization process involves divestiture, in the sense of shedding one's previous self-conception and taking on a new view of self that reflects one's role and membership in the new group (Van Maanen and Schein, 1979). We found that nearly a third of our respondents agreed with the statement that graduate school was changing them in ways they did not like. We cannot tell, of course, from our survey data whether they were experiencing major changes in identity or relatively minor changes in attitudes, beliefs, or behavior. We found our respondents about evenly split between those who agreed and those who disagreed that graduate school had positively reinforced their prior values, self-image, and way of thinking about the world. This item represents something of a converse to divestiture; that nearly half of these students disagreed that their prior basic concepts had been reinforced supports the conclusion that graduate school has considerable strength as a change process of the most fundamental kind, for better or for worse.

How Do Doctoral Students View Their Future Degree Completion and Career?

Our respondents were particularly optimistic about their chances of completing their degree (see Table 1.5). Ninety-four percent were very or somewhat certain that they would finish. This level of certainty probably reflects our decision not to include any first-year doctoral students in our sample; clearly those students are much less certain of their direction and progress. When we put the question a bit differently, asking whether students thought they had the ability to complete the graduate program with no trouble, we still found that over 80 percent replied affirmatively.

Looking beyond graduation to their career, our students were optimistic that the preparation they were receiving would serve them well: 84 percent

Table 1.5. Reflections on Graduate School and Academic Careers

	Very Certain	Somewhat Certain	Not Very Certain	I Doubt That I Will Finish
How certain are you that you will complete the Ph.D. degree?	72 percent	22 percent	5 percent	2 percent

	Strongly Agree	Agree	Disagree	Strongly Disagree
I know that I have the ability to get through my graduate program with no trouble.	32 percent	49 percent	17 percent	3 percent
My graduate school experiences will prepare me for the demands of my career.	22	62	13	3
Making it in my field depends a lot on whom you know.	16	5329	3	
Becoming a successful scientist depends as much on luck and chance as on ability and hard work.	16	39	35	11
I sometimes think that entering a doctoral program in this field was a mistake.	8	29	33	30
I would rather be in this program than doing anything else at this point in my life.	15	41	31	13

Note: Percentages may not add to 100 due to rounding.

Source: Acadia Institute Project on Professional Values and Ethical Issues in the Graduate Education of Scientists and Engineers.

thought that their graduate school experiences would prepare them for the demands of their prospective career. We also found, however, that students were aware that factors other than sheer ability might come into play in their career. Nearly 70 percent agreed that "making it" in their field depends a lot on whom you know. Perhaps more surprising is that 55 percent agreed that becoming a successful scientist (or social scientist or civil engineer) depends as much on luck and chance as on ability and hard work. Whether our respondents were taking into account the serendipity that is associated with major breakthroughs in research or the perceived uncertainties of academic or other employment is uncertain.

Finally, we presented students with two items that captured their overall reaction to their graduate experiences. On the negative side, over a third of the students admitted that they sometimes felt that entering their doctoral program was a mistake. Given these students' certainty that they would complete their work, such uncertainty about the initial decision could simply represent a normal reaction to a bad day, or it could reflect more troublesome issues in their graduate experience or uncertainty and worries about their future career path. On the positive side, over half of our respondents agreed that they would rather be in their doctoral program than doing anything else at that point in their life. That so many students could respond so positively to so strong a statement attests to the commitment that many students have to their graduate work and to the careers that will follow.

Discussion

This chapter provides an overview of students' perceptions of their experiences in doctoral programs. Our data, it is important to bear in mind, were collected in 1989 and are limited to the responses of students in four disciplines at major research universities. Nonetheless, we believe that our findings may be useful in suggesting how the graduate experience can be improved for many students, not in terms of curricular reform or other major programmatic changes but rather regarding the everyday ways in which students are taught, socialized, and prepared for careers. In thinking about these findings—and remembering our own graduate student days—we recognize that just because students think something is problematic does not necessarily mean that it needs fixing. Not all aspects of graduate education can or should be made pleasant. Graduate school simply involves a great deal of hard work. Our data do indicate, however, that substantial numbers of students are having experiences that could be substantially improved, both with respect to the quality of their education and the longer term effects on their professional socialization.

Based on the findings presented in this chapter, we highlight a few issues worthy of further scrutiny. First, we suggest that greater attention should be given to supervision and training of teaching assistants and research assistants. Many graduate students are interested in careers that include teaching. Despite the pervasive undervaluation of teaching in the reward system of major research institutions, today's students are the major pool from which tomorrow's faculty will be recruited to teach and train a new generation.

Second, student evaluations and faculty expectations for student performance are aspects of the graduate experience that many students find less than satisfactory. Students' expressed skepticism about the effectiveness of evaluation suggests that the certification component of graduate education may not function well enough to be reliable.

Third, we suggest that the department-level experiences of graduate students, reflected here in our analyses of departmental climates, would be fruitful avenues for further research on the graduate experience. Examination of departments as environments for graduate education might lead to suggestions of how faculty can change policies, requirements, and expectations to affect their students' experiences for the better.

Finally, we find grounds for concern in and a need for more detailed understanding of student reports that graduate school is changing them in ways they do not like. What changes do they feel they are undergoing and why? Do they view these changes as transient, situational adjustments or more lasting consequences of their graduate training and socialization?

Graduate school faculty and administrators can, and we believe should, periodically assess the experiences over time of students in their departments and programs and take remedial actions when problem areas are identified. Unfortunately, graduate programs cannot rely on advisors or mentors to handle problem areas. As other publications derived from the Acadia study show, graduate-student advising and what is glibly termed "mentoring" are often woefully inadequate (Swazey and Anderson, 1996; Anderson and Oju, in press). Rather, faculty members collectively and individually have a responsibility for improving the experiences of their graduate students. The costs of educating a doctoral student and preparing him or her for a postdoctoral career are very high. Every student who quits graduate school or otherwise fails to realize the benefits of graduate education productively—whether as a result of experiences that should never have happened or that should have been much better—represents a significant loss to the enterprise.

Notes

1. The Acadia Institute's Project on Professional Values and Ethical Issues in the Graduate Education of Scientists and Engineers was cosponsored by the American Academy for the Advancement of Science's Committee on Scientific Freedom and Responsibility, the Council of Graduate Schools, and Sigma Xi. It was supported by Grants No. 8913159 and 9222889 from the National Science Foundation. The following NSF components provided funding to the NSF Ethics and Values Studies Program for support of the project: the Directorate for Social, Behavioral, and Economic Sciences; the Directorate for Biological Sciences; the Directorate for Engineering; the Directorate for Mathematical and Physical Sciences; and the Office of the Inspector General. Opinions, findings, conclusions, and recommendations are the authors' and do not necessarily reflect the views of the National Science Foundation. The authors also gratefully acknowledge support from the Spencer Foundation.

2. The surveys that we sent to students and faculty in chemistry and microbiology referred to "scientists." Those sent to sociologists and civil engineers referred to "social scientists" and "civil engineers," respectively. Items presented in tables here show only the first wording.

References

Anderson, M. S. "Collaboration, the Doctoral Experience, and the Departmental Environment." *Review of Higher Education,* 1996a, *19*(3), 305–326.

Anderson, M. S. "Misconduct and Departmental Context: Evidence from the Acadia Institute's Graduate Education Project." *Journal of Information Ethics,* 1996b, 5 (1), 15–33.

Anderson, M. S., and Louis, K. S. "The Graduate Student Experience and Subscription to the Norms of Science." *Research in Higher Education,* 1994, *35* (3), 273–299.

Anderson, M. S., Louis, K. S., and Earle, J. "Disciplinary and Departmental Effects on Observations of Faculty and Graduate Student Misconduct." *Journal of Higher Education,* 1994, *65* (3), 331–350.

Anderson, M. S., and Oju, E. C. "Help from Faculty: Findings from the Acadia Institute Graduate Education Study" (working title). In G. C. Roberts and R. L. Sprague (eds.), *Mentoring for Research Values: The Forgotten Factor* (working title). Champaign: University of Illinois Press, in press.

Baird, L. L. "The Melancholy of Anatomy: The Personal and Professional Development of Graduate and Professional School Students." In J. M. Smart (ed.), *Higher Education: Handbook of Theory and Research.* Vol. 6. New York: Agathon Press, 1990.

Louis, K. S., Anderson, M. S., and Rosenberg, L. "Academic Misconduct and Values: The Department's Influence." *Review of Higher Education,* 1995, *18* (4), 393–422.

Swazey, J. P., and Anderson, M. S. *Mentors, Advisors and Role Models in Graduate and Professional Education.* Washington, D.C.: Association of Academic Health Centers, 1996. (To be reprinted in *Managing the Academic Health Center Mission: The Search for Integration.* Washington, D.C.: Association of Academic Health Centers, 1998.)

Swazey, J. P., Anderson, M. S., and Louis, K. S. "Ethical Problems in Academic Research." *American Scientist,* 1993, *81* (Nov./Dec.), 542–553.

Van Maanen, J., and Schein, E. H. "Toward a Theory of Organizational Socialization." In B. Staw (ed.), *Research in Organizational Behavior.* Vol. 1. Greenwich, Conn.: JAI Press, 1979.

MELISSA S. ANDERSON *is associate professor of higher education at the University of Minnesota. Her current research includes the Academic Life Project (an NSF-funded longitudinal study of the doctoral experience), as well as continuing work on academic-industry relationships and faculty demography in academic departments.*

JUDITH P. SWAZEY *is president of the Acadia Institute in Bar Harbor, Maine, a nonprofit center for the study of issues at the interfaces of science, medicine, and society. She was principal investigator for the institute's study of professional values and ethical issues in the graduate education of scientists and engineers.*

Some gifted writers have given their views on what it takes to be a graduate student—and what it gives.

"Grand Possibilities and Perilous Business": Academic Autobiographers on Graduate Education

Steven Weiland

Now well known for his contributions to the "interpretive turn" in the social and behavioral sciences, anthropologist Clifford Geertz (1995) recalls from his experience at Harvard in the 1950s the circumstances—still familiar today—of new graduate students who relish the scale and variety of the large research university even as they recognize the difficulties it presents.

> Finding one's way through this maze of grand possibilities, only loosely related, and some even in fairly serious tension with one another, was, however exciting (and it was enormously exciting), a perilous business. With so many ways to turn, so few tracks laid down, and so little experience of one's own to go by, even small decisions, to take this seminar, attack that subject, work with this professor, seemed enormously consequential—a reverseless commitment to something immense, portentous, splendid, and unclear. [p. 101]

Like many other scholars, Geertz reflects on his apprenticeship in order to probe the meanings of the academic vocation, its pleasures and trials. There is now abundant autobiographical reflection on faculty work. Recent collections of essays in this vein are typically based on disciplinary interests; some represent characteristics of a particular group of professors, like those coming from working-class backgrounds (Berger, 1990; Breit and Spencer, 1993; Cyr and Reich, 1996; Dews and Law, 1995; Fowler and Hardesty, 1994; Goetting and Fenstermacher, 1995; Karnos and Shoemaker, 1993; Keller, 1994; Kruzel and Rosenau, 1989; Neumann and Peterson, 1996; Orlans and Wallace, 1994; Veeser, 1996).

NEW DIRECTIONS FOR HIGHER EDUCATION, no. 101, Spring 1998 © Jossey-Bass Publishers

Indeed, the recent trend toward academic autobiography and personal dimensions of scholarship has prompted skepticism about the premises and results of both (for example, Patai, 1994; Simpson, 1996). I share this skepticism, though in previous work I have argued for greater attention to personal narratives for understanding academic careers (Weiland, 1994, 1995). We can learn much from autobiography about what motivates teachers and scholars, and about the conditions and meanings of their work, without accepting the argument that there is nothing to be said in scholarship that does not derive from personal history and subjectivity (Breit, 1987).

In what follows I gather personal reflections on the highs and lows (to state Geertz's pair from my title in a more vernacular spirit) of graduate education. My sampler does not, of course, exhaust such experiences and their meanings; and however valuable firsthand testimony of human experience is, there are plain problems associated with autobiography, academic or any other kind. Geertz (1995) identifies them when he reminds us that "nobody's under oath in autobiography, whose purpose is normally to keep an illusion in place" (p. 109). Retrospective accounts are both records and interpretations of experience. Academic autobiographers can contribute to developmental frameworks for graduate education (for example, Baird, 1990) and thus help us to understand how it is made part of an academic identity. In a brief conclusion, I propose what such narratives offer to us and to succeeding academic generations.

Telling Tales Out of (Graduate) School

Not surprisingly, as a genre, academic autobiography is dominated by writers in the humanities and social sciences, as these are the fields in which narrative forms are most welcome. Even so, not all recent academic autobiographers make graduate education central to their reflections about their academic identity (for example, Krupat, 1996). For those who do, memory yields recognition of the significance of formative academic experience in several categories: the influence of teachers, the formulation of scholarly purposes and projects, the challenges to expectations, the meanings of social class, and the overcoming of personal and institutional obstacles.

"In the Presence of the Great." The famed cognitive psychologist Jerome Bruner supplies a telling image of graduate study, indeed the one that dominates most accounts. He reports walking on the Harvard campus in 1938 and feeling himself to be "in the presence of the great." Added to that were "the towering elms, the oddly pleasing mix of architectural styles, the to me 'pure' scholars walking the crisscross paths under the trees. This was Athens and I was walking across the Agora." Harvard appealed to Bruner's snobbery, he confesses, but the many faculty luminaries made it "the place where the future of psychology was being shaped" (Bruner, 1983, p. 32).

Models of achievement and professional commitment were abundant. That the wide-ranging personality theorists Henry Murray and Gordon Allport, each of whom in his own way promoted narrative inquiry, did not have a "deep effect" on Bruner's thinking when he was a graduate student only reminds us that a career can evolve in unforseen ways. At the time he thought their work—and whatever advantages it presented for knowing about the "full person"—was limited by the habits of that period's personality inquiry (for example, the mechanically applied "trait" theory). "I wanted something more daring, some penetrating principle that would simplify, would render the surface complexity into something like a crystal" (p. 36). The task, then and now, was to translate being "in the presence of the great" into graduate work on new and potentially great ideas and methods.

Bruner was attracted to Department Chair Edward Boring, a historian of psychology also renowned for the rigor of his work habits and thought. "It was," Bruner remembers with painful satisfaction, "from Boring that I had the hardest time declaring my independence—a demanding Quaker father impossible to please" (p. 38). In effect, it was what might be called a complex dialectic of influence that was at the core of Bruner's graduate school years. Professors presented competing images of achievement, and in Bruner's mind and early professional identity was the opportunity to make an academic self from a sense of difference from an inspiring mentor. Records of influence of this kind abound in academic narratives (see Weiland, 1994, 1997) and, to complement Bruner on Boring, often include surprising evidence of the benevolence of scholars not otherwise known for such a quality. The autobiographical accounts of women who pioneered, often painfully, as graduate students in the 1960s in Berkeley's sociology department (Orlans and Wallace, 1994) offer, in stories of Erving Goffman carrying out the role of graduate advisor, reasons to rethink academic stereotypes.

To be sure, graduate study is built around the hierarchy of expert knowledge. But is there a graduate student who has not felt inadequate—in the presence of persons smarter and better prepared—not only before famous professors but also before other students? Astrophysicist Marc Davis remembers that "by the time I had gotten through my senior year at MIT, I was doing pretty well. My grades were good, and I applied to a bunch of graduate schools. When I went to Princeton in 1969 I encountered culture shock. I thought I knew physics, but here the class was full of people that were just unbelievable" (Lightman and Brawer, 1990, p. 345). So, too, was John Huchra, another cosmologist, uncertain of his prospects when he entered the California Institute of Technology in 1970, where he found himself "intimidated from the word go." Despite his qualifications and high grades he "figured [he] was a dummy" and not as good as the others in his classes (Lightman and Brawer, 1990, p. 381–382). Both succeeded because personal modesty became a resource for scientific ambition.

"Disinvesting" and "Taking the Heat." There was apparently little self-doubt, at least at the outset, when Gary Becker went to the University of Chicago in the 1950s to study economics. Milton Friedman had joined the faculty just a few years before, its second choice after it could not get the well-published economist it wanted. Of course, Friedman soon achieved a scholarly record any professor would envy, but Becker claims that Friedman would have been enormously influential on graduate students even if he had published much less.

Friedman taught a two-quarter sequence on price theory, required for all economics graduate students. According to Becker, Friedman was "at his best" balancing theory and example. "These applications helped students absorb [his] vision of economics as a tool for understanding the real world, not as a game played by clever academics" (Becker, 1990, p. 141). Friedman was an intense and demanding teacher, with high standards and sometimes little patience, but he invariably helped those who were struggling. Becker learned more than economics from Friedman. He came to know himself better and his own academic aspirations and capacities.

Becker had arrived at graduate school secure in his knowledge of mathematical applications in economics. He was readying his first articles for publication. Thus, he was gratified when told that he need not fulfill the prerequisite for Friedman's course—but he resisted even that requirement. Although his advisor "handled the ignorance of a twenty-year-old gently," Becker went to Friedman's first class in a skeptical mood.

> After fifteen or twenty minutes he asked a question, my hand shot up, he called on me, and I gave an answer. Forty years later I remember his response: "That was not an answer but merely restated the question in different words." I felt humiliated, but I knew he was right, and I was much impressed by his quick and correct evaluation of my answer. I remained silent the rest of the class while Friedman gave an excellent lecture. [pp. 141–142]

The articles would now wait as Becker realized that he "should spend the next few years investing in new knowledge and disinvesting misperceptions" (p. 142). Becker's first professional publication (five years later) was coauthored with Friedman.

Speaking of the nature of graduate education today, Becker claims that economics is too much like physics and chemistry. From this perspective, he identifies why Friedman made such a durable impression on him. "The problem is that many economists teaching theory are not confident that it is very helpful in understanding behavior. And their lack of confidence in its relevance is absorbed by students" (p. 142). Thus, graduate students are in debt to their teachers for both (at least a good part of) what they know and what they do not (but should).

Becker achieved not only theoretical sophistication but also a kind of institutional solidarity as a graduate student. Friedman and his colleagues, leaders of the so-called "Chicago School," offered a unique approach to their subject. "Some students found this conflict with most of the profession difficult to handle, but others developed a chip on their shoulder and became aggressively proud of being Chicagoans" (p. 143). True enough, Becker acknowledges, their aggressiveness sometimes made them unwelcome colleagues at other institutions, but Becker absorbed what he could from his experience, including what might be called the aggressiveness of Friedman himself as a critic of dissertations.

> Some top students shied away from working with Friedman because they could not take the heat: they could not handle psychologically his sharp and blunt criticisms and his quick insights. In essence they feared being overwhelmed intellectually. I also had these fears but managed to control them enough to recognize how much I could learn from him. [p. 144]

There is some consolation in Becker's memory that Friedman was even harder on visiting scholars.

Friedman was always a zealot and missionary. "He tried first to find the truth and then to convert others" (p. 146). For Friedman, embarrassed or even psychologically "wounded" students were a price that had to be paid for rigorous academic preparation.

Not surprisingly, Becker has had a successful career as a teacher and scholar, as have had many of Friedman's other students. Hardened as he was by his mentor, Becker nevertheless says he wished Friedman had had a more variable touch in his intellectual relations, sometimes recognizing a role for face-saving for those whose projects did not (at least at the time he encountered them) meet his high standards. Would Friedman have been as effective a teacher had he been so? Would he have had the same lasting impact on his students? Such questions ultimately matter less to Becker than the satisfactions of intellectual deference. "I continue to be grateful that I was wise enough—and lucky enough—to come to Chicago and to spend six years studying at Friedman's feet" (p. 146).

"My Own Solitary Utopian Community." At twenty, Michael Zuckerman wanted to be a novelist, perhaps because he had been educated by his mother in "the ethos and arcana of elite culture" and being a writer was yet another way to move far beyond his parents' immigrant roots. "[The rest of the family and I] were as keen to shed the encumbrances of old country identities as she was" (Zuckerman, 1993, p. 5). He produced a novella (unpublished) but soon thereafter entered graduate school at Harvard in American Studies, thinking that creative and academic work could be combined. He was immediately influenced by the example of Murray Murphey, and became one of a "blessed band" that took up his ambitious intellectual project. "We would help him accomplish the end he put so palpably before us, of unriddling the mysteries of the American character." The peculiar appeal of the work of his graduate school cohort was the chance (they thought) to forge a new discipline. "We would be anthropologists of a nation state, historical psychologists of a complex culture" (p. 5).

In a sense, Zuckerman's part in this great project can be traced to an accident. His memory reveals how contingent yet fruitful the graduate classroom can be. As he shows, finding himself as a first-year student sitting on the wrong side of Bernard Bailyn in his renowned graduate seminar in early American history had lifelong consequences. When Bailyn went around the seminar table inviting students to identify essay topics they had chosen from the list he had supplied, Zuckerman went last and found that the only ones he was interested in had already been selected. Those that were left "appeared arid beyond any plausible pedagogic purpose" (p. 6). Stuck now with a commitment to study voting procedures in eighteenth-century Massachusetts, Zuckerman describes his initial efforts as "desultory as they were desperate." When he reconceptualized the problem in keeping with the grand intellectual commitment he had made to Murphey, however, he "dug into [the subject] like a man possessed" (p. 7).

Zuckerman says that he "did not fathom his fervor" then and can barely do so now as a middle-aged professor. "Scientists have written of their experience in certain collaborative enterprises—the Manhattan Project, for example—as utopian. I had, in the sudden intensity of my research, my own solitary utopian community" (p. 7). Thus, he "tore through," "devoured," and "ransacked" the records and texts for his study. He was "seized" by his subject and felt a "creative frenzy" unlike any he had experienced before as a student or budding novelist. "I sensed myself at the threshold of another world. . . . A culture was coming to life before my astonished eyes" (p. 7). The excitement of original scholarly work is difficult to convey to a skeptical public who views academic specialization as a drain on teaching. Above all, Zuckerman's approach to his graduate research turns out to have significant moral consequences. "I had to listen to voices and values that were not my own yet possessed an integrity and passion that required recognition if my research and writing were to be satisfying" (p. 8).

From within a historical and scholarly problem pursued with zeal, and with a sense that the stakes were high in undertaking foundational criticism of American society, Zuckerman transformed an early ambivalence about graduate study into unceasing dedication. He confesses, "As I began my graduate study, that mission and that vision were not the main motives that drove me. It would be silly to say they were. More than I sought scholarly success, I wanted the free time I fancied that scholars had." This turns out to be an "inane calculation." Luckily, Murphey helps, too, by educating Zuckerman in doing faculty work. That unexpected part of the graduate curriculum "gave me my first glimpses of the academic routines that still fill my days, for better or for worse" (p. 6).

"It Was Love That Had Brought Us There." Zuckerman remembers only the pleasure of graduate education, but for Jane Tompkins, memory yields contrasting emotions. "My mind goes straight to the incidents marked by pain and isolation—incidents united to each other by a sense of laborious, desperate striving to achieve barely attainable goals. . . .The work, the difficulty of the work, sucked up all my energy and attention, and I tended to ignore the sources of solace and comfort that were available. Human love and companionship were set at a discount because my fear of not succeeding was so great" (Tompkins 1996, p. 74).

Aspiration and desire were the attributes she brought to her graduate studies in English at Yale, also in the early 1960s. Such motives also guided the performance of other students but in ways that made them, in her view, more fearful and thus more competitive than they needed to be. They were afraid to appear ignorant and to make plain what had made them want to study literature in the first place. For her the reason is clear:

> It was love that had brought us there, students and professors alike, but to lis-
> ten to us talk you would never have known it. The love didn't have a conjuga-
> tion or a declension; it couldn't be articulated as a theory or contained in a body
> of information. It wasn't intellectual—that was the shameful thing—though it
> had an intellectual dimension. Being amorphous, tremulous, pulsing, it was
> completely vulnerable. So we all hid it as best we could, and quite successfully
> most of the time. [p. 79]

Perhaps it was the shared (but unstated) view that gaining a Yale Ph.D. would mean lifelong membership in a "select company" of people who appreciated "the power of language to create worlds that corresponded to the loftiest human aspirations" (p. 76). Moreover, and more in keeping with the period and intellectual resistance to it, "going to graduate school and studying literature for me stood in direct opposition to the mode of life represented by the stationwagon people: suburban, conventional, materialistic, without imagination, sensitivity, or appreciation of the finer things in life. Graduate school was going to give me the means to rise above all that and achieve something special" (p. 76).

Tompkins grants that she was idealistic and ignorant, a combination that she believes still often shapes the hopes and expectations of many graduate students. "It was an expression of love and the best thing I had to offer." Thus, Tompkins's recent declaration of her intention to leave Duke and academic life is poignant even though predictable from her graduate school years: "At Yale I spent five years learning how to strangle my love, and I never quite got over it" (p. 76).

"C'est Bien." Between Zuckerman's pleasure and Tompkins's pain there is surely the ambivalent experience of many graduate students whose motives are uncertain even if their performance turns out to be exemplary. Something of this uncertainty is observable in the most widely read academic autobiography in recent years, Alice Kaplan's *French Lessons* (1993). Kaplan arrived in New Haven in the mid-1970s to study French when much had changed in graduate education in the humanities, at Yale and elsewhere. Literary study, in English and other Western languages, was dominated by a group of topics and questions identified under the heading of "theory." In particular, Yale achieved fame as the home of Deconstruction, a French import guided by the ideas of Jacques Derrida.

Kaplan had come to graduate school with an unusually intense love of French, but that did not mean that her experience did not jeopardize her commitments. True enough, to be at Yale was to be at the center of things, but it was also to face the pressures of theoretical and pedagogical change as expressed in conflicted relations between students, and between students and professors. We are a long way from the Emerson Hall of Bruner's graduate school cohort, where "debate was incessant and good natured among graduate students, and the sharing of interests was cordial and genuine" (Bruner 1983, p. 33). Kaplan's fellow graduate students are not without their own version of collegiality, but it is often based more on shared anxiety about the poor job market than on genial habits of intellectual discourse.

Kaplan enrolled in the classes of the enigmatic Paul deMan, who was to many students an intellectual inspiration even if he resisted most aspects of the standard role of graduate school mentor. In the seminar room deMan abjured conventional relations even as he (paradoxically and in the manner of Deconstruction) deepened them.

> After a student made a comment, he muttered "bien"—well done. As soon as he said it, he got that wistful smile on his face and he apologized, saying how much he hated the set-up where the student waits for the teacher to say "bien," like a dog waiting for a bone. When I first thought about it I felt grateful to him for refusing to manipulate us but later I got mad: the way he told it, we were just eager dogs, needy and vulnerable. Did he think we would scrounge for any scrap? [p. 152]

But students change and Kaplan records her growing confidence in her work, deriving (no doubt to deMan's satisfaction even if unregistered) from the high standards and frosty attitudes displayed by the faculty.

> I had been so hesitant a student, and now, at the dissertation phase, was the sea change. I was a "late bloomer." I knew what I wanted to write; I was writing my own voice. [Her advisor] read my pages faster and faster as I went on; after six months he said, "this is good." "C'est bien." I didn't feel like a dog scrounging for a bone, I felt great. [p. 161]

When she completed her dissertation and there was a disagreement about whether or not it deserved special recognition, she decided that "their argument was my prize" (p. 164).

Class in the Graduate Classroom. Kaplan's middle-class background—the educational attainments of her parents and the financial resources available to her—helped to make her evolving vocation possible. Rosa Maria Pegueros is a Mexican American who grew up in the Salvadoran immigrant community in San Francisco. Her working-class family life meant economic hardship and constraints on educational opportunities. Bewildered by her love of books, her father once said, "I worry about you. You have no ambition; all you want to do is read" (Pegueros 1995, p. 91). Social class made a difference at every level of schooling, and even though her bookish habits led to a college degree (in philosophy), graduate school hardly figured in her plans, however much she desired it.

If you aspire to something more than just making a working-class living, then pulling yourself up by the bootstraps rarely suffices by itself. I was fooled into believing that equality was the logical by-product of higher education. Now that I have become a university professor, with far more education than anyone from home, I struggle with the task of reconciling the standards expected of academics with my own values. [p. 97]

In the years following her B.A., Pegueros earned a law degree but found legal practice unsatisfying. A ten-year career in social work followed. In her late thirties, Pegueros entered the graduate program in Latin American history at the University of California at Los Angeles. Her first and chief disappointment was being treated as a child, "infantilized" as she puts it, when professors and administrators alike could not recognize what her experience had already supplied to her emerging academic vocation. "I came back to school as a confident adult, secure in my ability to manage a life balanced between work and love, only to have my priorities questioned and even displaced by a profession that places little importance on being a successful *person*" (p. 100; emphasis in original). She claims that those already part of university culture "forget that success is predicated not only on native ability and hard work but also on a supportive home environment and a hospitable atmosphere at school" (p. 101).

For Pegueros and others like her, advanced study can unreasonably demand more than is available to otherwise intelligent and articulate graduate students. Julie Charlip, who also pursued a Ph.D. in history at UCLA, says, "Graduate school is about more than what you know. . . . The problem isn't knowing the material in class but knowing the references made over cappuccino" (Charlip, 1995, p. 38).

Pegueros focuses mainly on the obstacles facing working-class graduate students. Others sharing her perspective have made different themes central to their autobiographies. For example, Naton Leslie (1995) worked in carpentry prior to graduate study and drew important lessons from it.

A cabinetmaker once told me that a good carpenter works just beyond the capacity of his tools. He said that a particular cut or joint was easy to make if you had exactly the required tools: the tools simply functioned as required, and the job was accomplished. A good carpenter, however, has to do things for which the perfect tools aren't available, adding skill, a steady hand, and good eye, a fine touch with a rasp. Setting dowels without a drill press, cutting rabbet joints without a table saw—that's what marked a fine carpenter. And that's exactly what I did [in graduate study in writing] at Ohio University. [p. 72]

Graduate students with working-class backgrounds have a keen sense of social injustice, the irony of their professional circumstances, and the everyday peculiarities of the academic vocations. Thus, sociologist John Sumser (1995) says (and confirms the experience of Leslie) that "the key to the impact of working-class backgrounds on intellectuals is located not in the idea of class but in the idea of working" (p. 299).

"The Pain Is Fleeting. It's Part of Life." Like Rosa Pegueros, Patricia Schmidt began graduate study after considerable professional experience, in her case as a high school teacher. She returned first for part-time, then full-time study in education at New York University over the objections of her husband and after battling alcoholism and cancer. Also like Pegueros, her initial classroom encounters appeared to her to be disproportionately shaped by the authority of professors. With her experience and hardships as backdrop, she wanted desperately to "take responsibility for learning."

Schmidt's autobiography is an unusual one for its intimacy and the extent to which it reveals how close textual work can be understood as a format for how graduate students not only study subjects but themselves too. In Schmidt's case it is "reader response" theory in literary studies and its impact on teaching at all levels of education. Both features of her account are observable from her graduate school diary, excerpts of which appear in her book (I have combined entries from the first year of her degree program):

> Talked to Mary today—the nightmares we all share, the freeing of the self. I raised my hand today to get out of self will and self fear. . . . I guess I still want to teach, love working with people, just abhor the politics of academic life. Do potters have political hegemonies? Probably. Stick to what you know! . . . My proposal needs much more work than I'd thought. It seems insurmountable but it will work itself out. . . . It's all in God's hands and I'll be fine (after the pain). After the pain. The pain is fleeting. It's part of life. . . . So, is [my project] a phenomenological study of dialogic pedagogy? What is that? . . . It's so ironic that we're encouraged to experiment, to "construct" our own meaning and here we are falling into predictable paradigms. . . . Rites of passage. So, Pat go within. [Schmidt, 1997, pp. 138–148 *passim*]

To these internal difficulties is added the need to work closely with inhospitable history graduate students in a project aimed at improving undergraduate writing. The chief problem is a familiar one—the status of students in education in relation to those in the disciplines of the arts and sciences. The rivalries are intense and Schmidt admits now to having less compassion than she would have liked for her less experienced (but still arrogant) colleagues. Still, Schmidt says, mindful of the structure of graduate school when students are often (silently but effectively) asked to defer to professors and to the conventional goals of academic projects: "It is amazing how life goes when we have principles we believe in and actually try to live in and with and by" (p. 145).

To paraphrase a recent popular political slogan, "it's the motivation" when considering the essentials of satisfying graduate study. In today's problematic academic job market, with the ethical dilemmas it poses (Nelson, 1997), only the love of subjects and a strong wish to do the work can explain the cheerful accounts of students included in a new comprehensive guide to graduate education in the humanities and social sciences (Lingua Franca 1997).

Schmidt's story ends with the planning for her dissertation (what was to become her autobiography). Humiliated, in her view, by a senior professor who was acting largely out of antipathy to Schimdt's newly revised and more personal authorial voice, she persists in a way familiar to all writers: "I took the advice that was useful and helpful and let go of the rest" (p. 148). Speaking for academic autobiographers generally in their memories of graduate education and other experiences, she concludes: "I have had powerful reading and learning experiences, but none of the standard or traditional assessments comes close to measuring or describing the deep, personal knowledge learners have. I have watched the transformations in my students' lives and I know this deeply in my own life" (pp. 133–134).

Conclusion: The Narrative and the Generative

Not all accounts of graduate education aspire to deep knowledge of living and learning, but the many that do reveal how autobiographers find meaning in their academic apprenticeship. Why tell tales of graduate school if not to show that embracing scientific or intellectual values is also a path to self-knowledge? If "narrating the self in adulthood" means the achievement of "unity" and "purpose" in life and work (McAdams, 1996), the representation of graduate education in academic autobiography can be understood as a sign of how durable apprenticeship is to professorial identity. That includes the wish to address succeeding generations of scholars and scientists via narratives in a professional voice modified by personal motives.

Not surprisingly, there is in academic autobiography a strong generative impulse, that is, the wish to have a role, in Erik Erikson's phrase, in "establishing and guiding the next generation" (Erikson, 1963, p. 267). Academic autobiographers invariably focus on what was given to them by their teachers when they were graduate students. Now they speak as teachers themselves. For those reading their work—whether in careers or anticipating them—there is recognition that graduate education, even if its virtues are sometimes (to return to Geertz) "obscure," is also often "splendid."

References

Baird, L. "The Melancholy of Anatomy: The Personal and Professional Development of Graduate and Professional School Students." In J. C. Smart (ed.), *Higher Education: Handbook of Theory and Research*. Vol. 6. New York: Agathon Press, 1990.

Becker, G. "Milton Friedman." In E. Shils (ed.), *Remembering the University of Chicago: Teachers, Scientists, and Scholars*. Chicago: University of Chicago Press, 1990.

Berger, B. (ed.). *Authors of Their Own Lives: Intellectual Autobiographies by Twenty American Sociologists*. Berkeley: University of California Press, 1990.

Breit, W. "Biography and the Making of Economic Worlds." *Southern Economic Journal,* 1987, 53, 823–833.

Breit, W., and Spencer, R. (eds.). *Lives of the Laureates: Thirteen Nobel Economists*. Cambridge, Mass.: MIT Press, 1993.

Bruner, J. *In Search of Mind: Essays in Autobiography*. New York: HarperCollins, 1983.

Charlip, J. "A Real Class Act: Searching for Identity in the 'Classless' Society." In C. L. Dews and C. L. Law (eds.), *This Fine Place So Far from Home: Voices of Academics from the Working Class.* Philadelphia: Temple University Press, 1995.

Cyr, D., and Reich, B. (eds.). "Scaling the Ivory Tower: Stories from Women in Business School Faculties." Westport, Conn.: Praeger, 1996.

Dews, C. L., and Law, C. L. (eds.). *This Fine Place So Far from Home: Voices of Academics from the Working Class.* Philadelphia: Temple University Press, 1995.

Erikson, E. H. *Childhood and Society.* New York: Norton, 1963.

Fowler, D., and Hardesty, D. (eds.). *Others Knowing Others: Perspectives on Ethnographic Careers.* Washington, D.C.: Smithsonian Institution Press, 1994.

Geertz, C. *After the Fact: Two Countries, Four Decades, One Anthropologist.* Cambridge, Mass.: Harvard University Press, 1995.

Goetting, A., and Fenstermacher, S. (eds.). *Individual Voices, Collective Visions: Fifty Years of Women in Sociology.* Philadelphia: Temple University Press, 1995.

Kaplan, A. *French Lessons: A Memoir.* Chicago: University of Chicago Press, 1993.

Karnos, D., and Shoemaker, R. (eds.). *Falling in Love with Wisdom: American Philosophers Talk About Their Calling.* New York: Oxford University Press, 1993.

Keller, P. (ed.). *Academic Paths: Career Decisions and Experiences of Psychologists.* Hillsdale, N.J.: Erlbaum, 1994.

Krupat, A. "A Nice Jewish Boy Among the Indians." In A. Krupat (ed.), *The Turn to the Native: Studies in Culture and Criticism.* Lincoln: University of Nebraska Press, 1996.

Kruzel, J., and Rosenau, J. (eds.). *Journeys Through World Politics: Autobiographical Reflections of Thirty-Four Academic Travelers.* Lexington, Mass.: Heath, 1989.

Leslie, N. "You Were Raised Better Than That." In C. L. Dews and C. L. Law. (eds.), *This Fine Place So Far from Home: Voices of Academics from the Working Class.* Philadelphia: Temple University Press, 1995.

Lightman, A., and Brawer, R. *Origins: The Lives and Worlds of Modern Cosmologists.* Cambridge, Mass.: Harvard University Press, 1990.

Lingua Franca. *The Real Guide to Grad School: What You Better Know Before You Choose.* New York: Lingua Franca Books, 1997.

McAdams, D. "Narrating the Self in Adulthood." In J. E. Birren and others (eds.), *Aging and Biography: Explorations in Adult Development.* New York: Springer, 1996.

Nelson, C. *Will Teach for Food: Academic Labor in Crisis.* Minneapolis: University of Minnesota Press, 1997.

Neumann, A., and Peterson, P. (eds.). *Learning from Our Lives: Women, Research, and Autobiography in Education.* New York: Teachers College Press, 1996.

Orlans, K., and Wallace, R. (eds.). *Gender and the Academic Experience: Berkeley Women Sociologists.* Lincoln: University of Nebraska Press, 1994.

Patai, D. "Sick and Tired of Scholars' Nouveau Solipsism." *Chronicle of Higher Education,* Feb. 23, 1994, p. A52.

Pegueros, R. "Todos Vuelven: From Potrero Hill to UCLA." In C. L. Dews and C. L. Law (eds.), *This Fine Place So Far from Home: Voices of Academics from the Working Class.* Philadelphia: Temple University Press, 1995.

Schmidt, P. *Beginning in Retrospect: Writing and Reading a Teacher's Life.* New York: Teachers College Press, 1997.

Simpson, D. "Speaking Personally: The Culture of Autobiographical Criticism." In H. A. Veeser (ed.), *Confessions of the Critics: North American Critics' Biographical Moves.* New York: Routledge, 1996.

Sumser, J. "Working It Out: Values, Perspectives, and Autobiography." In C. L. Dews and C. L. Law (eds.), *This Fine Place So Far from Home: Voices of Academics from the Working Class.* Philadelphia: Temple University Press, 1995.

Tompkins, J. *A Life in School: What the Teacher Learned.* Reading, Mass.: Addison-Wesley, 1996.

Veeser, H. A. (ed.). *Confessions of the Critics: North American Critics' Biographical Moves.* New York: Routledge, 1996.

Weiland, S. "Writing the Academic Life: Faculty Careers in Narrative Perspective." *Review of Higher Education,* 1994, *17,* 395–422.

Weiland, S. "Life History and Academic Work: The Career of 'Professor G.'" In R. Josselson and A. Lieblich (eds.), *The Narrative Study of Lives.* Vol. 3. Thousand Oaks, Calif.: Sage, 1995.

Weiland, S. "One Life 'After' Another: Identity, Influence and Academic Careers." *Centennial Review,* 1997, *41,* 251–290.

Zuckerman, M. *Almost Chosen People: Oblique Biographies in the American Grain.* Berkeley: University of California Press, 1993.

STEVEN WEILAND is professor of higher education and director of the Jewish Studies Program at Michigan State University, where he also teaches in the Department of English.

We can better prepare students for success in graduate school and beyond by making formal instruction in general professional skills a standard part of graduate training programs.

Survival Skills for Graduate School and Beyond

Beth A. Fischer, Michael J. Zigmond

Part of our responsibility toward graduate students is to provide them with a strong background in their field and to teach them how to design and carry out experiments. If, however, we are to ensure their success in graduate school and beyond, this is not enough. Students must also acquire many other "survival skills"—skills such as how to communicate their ideas and results, obtain jobs and funding, and attract students and staff (Bloom, 1992; Bird, 1994; National Academy of Sciences, 1995). In developing mechanisms for providing this training, faculty must make two key assumptions: one concerning the nature of the students' backgrounds when they enter the program, and the other regarding what awaits them when they leave. If the assumptions now being made are not correct, we may need to consider changing the nature of doctoral training.

Who are we training, and where do they go on graduation? A cursory examination of graduate training programs today suggests that doctoral students in the United States are a very heterogeneous group. Graduate school is no longer the exclusive province of native-born, unmarried, 22-year-old white males; many entering graduate students now are women, members of underrepresented minority groups, or students for whom English is not their native language. In addition, whereas it once may have been reasonable to assume that most doctoral students would secure tenure-stream positions at research universities soon after the completion of their dissertation, this is no longer the case.

We thank the National Science Foundation, the National Institute of Mental Health, and the University of Pittsburgh for their support of our Survival Skills and Ethics Project.

Among the students who received their doctoral degree in science and engineering in 1983–1986, only 43 percent are now in academia, a figure that includes both tenure-stream and non-tenure-stream positions in four-year colleges, universities, and medical schools (National Academy of Sciences, 1995). Although accurate statistics are hard to come by, one has the impression that the competition for many types of jobs has increased; certainly it often is very high. A single advertisement for a faculty position often is reported to generate some 250 responses, and notices of jobs in industry may result in a similar number of inquiries. Moreover, getting a job is only the beginning of the competitions that must be won.

In short, many of the students entering graduate school are unfamiliar with the culture of an American university, its jargon, and its conventions (Etzkowitz, Kemelgor, Neuschatz, and Uzzi, 1992). They may find themselves without peers to whom they can easily relate; they may have responsibilities to others that place strains on their time as well as their finances; and their interests, as well as the realities of the job market, may dictate that they will take a very different career track than that of their principal role model, the tenure-stream faculty member at a research university (National Academy of Sciences, 1995; Varmus, 1995). Thus, although there has always been a need for survival skills training, we believe that the recent changes in student populations and job opportunities dictate that even more attention should be paid to providing trainees with adequate instruction in these abilities.

The survival skills needed to succeed in graduate school and beyond can be divided into four categories: (1) basic skills, including how to be a successful graduate student; (2) communication skills, specifically, being able to convey the results of one's work through publications and oral presentations; (3) job skills, for finding and maintaining employment; and (4) advanced skills, including teaching, grant writing, and personnel management. Integral to each of these skills is a core survival skill, the ability to behave as a responsible professional. We base our recommendations concerning survival skills on our experiences with graduate students, particularly through our co-directorship of the University of Pittsburgh's Survival Skills and Ethics Program.

Basic Skills: Surviving Graduate School

Learning to Create

> When asked what the evidence was for a particular statement, the student said simply, "It's written in the textbook."

Although on the surface the transition from college to graduate school seems similar to the many steps in rank that have come before it, this transition is vastly different and requires a significant shift in attitude. To paraphrase Dr. Indira Nair of Carnegie-Mellon University: Throughout the pre-college and undergraduate years, students are primarily "consumers" of knowledge; however, during their graduate training, individuals are expected gradually to assume the role of "creators" of new knowledge. Thus, their tasks as graduate students are more similar to those of a practitioner than to those of traditional students: They must go beyond what is known, asking questions, seeking answers, and disseminating their results.

Furthermore, as part of their new role, graduate students must advance past the study skills that may have served them well in high school and college. They must learn to question assumptions and critically evaluate the literature rather than just memorize facts. In addition, graduate students must recognize that they are now, more than ever, responsible for the development of their own career. The attitude and motivation they bring to this process is crucial. Again, what is necessary is significantly different from what was required of them as undergraduates. The task is no longer to work hard enough to complete an externally imposed assignment and get a good grade. Graduate students need to realize that to become successful professionals, in many ways they must begin to set their own "assignments." Thus, they themselves, not the system, must push them to excel.

Think Ahead and Plan Backwards

> A fifth-year student in the biomedical sciences said, "I can't even begin to think about a postdoc until after I'm done with my thesis. I was planning on taking a month off then anyway— that should give me plenty of time."

Graduate school is a means to an end, not the end itself. Yet, many graduate students spend little time thinking about where they will be five to ten years after completion of their degree. High school led to college and college led to graduate school without too much independent planning. Traditionally, the goals seemed obvious—usually a tenure-track position at the research university—and the route seemed straightforward, too. Moreover, advisors, committees, and graduate requirements provided a safety net.

The graduate students of today need to confront the future more actively. They must begin by understanding the changes in career options, not in the negative sense of a "Ph.D. glut" but in the positive sense of broadened opportunities. They must come to appreciate the increased competition for jobs and resources. They must begin to set achievable long-term goals. Then, with their goals in mind, students should plan backwards—that is, plot out what they will need to learn and do in order to obtain and succeed in the position they desire, setting milestones to track their progress on the way. Indeed, planning with their goals in mind is an essential first step in taking an active role to ensure that their training program provides them with relevant and efficient preparation.

Choosing an Advisor

> One day a graduate student's advisor told her that he was going out of town for
> a week and that when he returned he expected her to be gone from his lab.
> When she expressed shock and indicated that she hadn't been warned of any
> problems during the two years she'd been in his lab, her advisor indicated that
> this was her own fault because she never asked if there were any problems. The
> student chose not to continue graduate studies.

One of the first tasks that a graduate student faces is frequently one of the most
critical—choosing an advisor. New graduate students may not realize the variables involved, the choices they have, or what they can (and cannot) expect
from a good advisor. In addition to talking to prospective faculty advisors, students also need to talk to present or former students of the faculty to find out
what their experiences have been.

Students need to be certain that their advisors are suitable and have a tem-
perament that is compatible with their own. All too often students are willing
to pursue work with a suboptimal advisor on the assumption that they can
tough it out for those five or so years of graduate study. Students need to recognize that their advisor will be an influential part of their career for many
years after the receipt of their degree. Letters of recommendation from one's
advisor are frequently required not just for obtaining employment, but for
securing grants and promotions as well. Thus, students should choose an advisor with the understanding that they will need to maintain a long-term relationship with that individual.

As part of the process of selecting an advisor, the trainee should take into consideration some critical variables, variables that may not be known to most incoming graduate students. These variables include the role of the student in generating
research questions; ownership of ideas and authorship on publications; financial
support for living expenses and travel to professional meetings; the amount of time
to be spent on research; and the definition of an adequate doctoral dissertation.
Investigating these issues at the outset helps to safeguard the trainee by protecting
the student from becoming invested in a research project, only to learn that their
advisor's policies are not compatible with their needs, with the result of being
forced to accept irksome policies or abandon their work to date on a project.

Finally, with regard to choosing an advisor, students need to realize that no
one person can satisfy all of their educational needs. For this reason, faculty
should encourage and students should seek to build a group of mentors who
can cumulatively address the needs of the trainee. This tactic may be particularly important for trainees who come from underrepresented populations and
are not be able to find adequate role models among the individuals in their field.

Developing a Plan of Study

> "I've been told that the best plan is to complete my thesis research before I hold
> my first committee meeting," said the student with some conviction. "That way

they won't be able to ask me to do something different from what I've planned, and I'll get out of here quicker."

The next step is to develop and get approved a plan for studies—whether such a plan is required or not. This plan should outline the courses that the individual will take and the examinations that are part of the milestones that students must pass to receive their degree. We encourage students to include the dates on which they will have completed each of these steps, setting interim deadlines as an aid to meeting those larger milestones that may be several years away. This also provides benchmarks for progress so that students can make adjustments along the way if necessary. In preparing the plan of study, students would do well to remember two principles: First, not all the rules that are written down need to be followed; second, not all the rules that must be followed are written down. Reading the graduate handbook is not enough. Students must talk with their graduate program's academic advisor, their own research advisor, and other students in the program.

Selecting a Dissertation Topic

"I'm interested in forest ecology," stated the graduate applicant. "I know that there aren't any faculty members here in that area, but that's okay. I already have experience in the field. All I want is a place to do my work and get a degree."

A thesis topic must deal with the testing of a hypothesis of interest to the student, the advisor, and a significant number of people in the field. Students will not be able to do their best work unless they find the issues they are studying to be compelling; advisors will not be able to provide adequate oversight unless the topic is of interest to them, too; and the final product will attract little attention if the matter at hand is not of interest to others in the field. Selecting a thesis that is driven by a hypothesis rather than being simply descriptive adds a further dimension to the level of interest it will generate. But one must take care not to set out to prove their hypothesis, but merely to test it; indeed, one should actually endeavor to disprove the hypothesis, tentatively accepting it when all efforts to disprove it have failed.

In selecting a topic for their research, students also need to consider the feasibility of the project (with regard to time and resources, available expertise, budget, and equipment). Students tend to propose to do too much for their dissertation, but this is the time to be conservative. There will be time to be more expansive after the plan has been approved. After all, no one has ever failed their thesis defense because they accomplished too much! Finally, students should choose a project that will be interesting enough to merit a Ph.D., whether the experiment "works" or not. That is, obtaining a degree should not be contingent on getting a certain result.

Establishing and Using an Advising Committee

> When advised that she should pick her thesis committee carefully, the student told us that this was not an issue at her institution, since committees were established for the students. When asked on what basis the committees were organized, she indicated that it seemed as though assignments were used to equalize the responsibilities of faculty members, since the faculty who were selected frequently had no students of their own and did little research. She was surprised to learn that this was not standard practice.

At some point in their graduate training, students must establish an advising committee. Sometimes this does not occur until it is time to propose a thesis topic, but we encourage students to form their committee within the first few weeks of graduate school. The committee can be modified as the student's interests change. In the meantime it provides a range of advice, the initial kernel of a professional network, a forum for informal presentations and discussions, and protection against the occasional overbearing advisor. Once the committee is formed, the students should provide members with regular progress reports and should call meetings every six months or so.

Communication Skills

Frequently, graduate students misjudge the importance of writing, speaking, and networking skills to the development of their career. Many students enter a research-oriented field because they are much more comfortable working with objects and data than they are with other people and descriptive prose. Yet communication skills are essential for researchers. Researchers must be able to communicate effectively with colleagues, professionals in other fields, policymakers, and the lay public. The need for communication skills has recently been underscored by documents such as *Reshaping the Graduate Education of Scientists and Engineers* (National Academy of Sciences, 1995), in which leaders from industry cite the importance of researchers being able communicate their results and interact effectively with nontechnical professionals.

Written Communication

> The student was surprised to learn that he would not get paid for publishing a research article. Moreover, when it was explained that he might even have to pay page charges, he was incredulous.

Frequently, students (and faculty) do not enjoy writing. They may not understand their responsibilities with regard to publishing, the conventions of writing technical documents, or even what the peer-review process entails. Yet, the ability to communicate effectively in writing is an extremely important skill, one that is often central to advancement as a professional. In addition to learning how to improve the quality of their writing, students also need to learn about the conventions of writing for publication, including how to determine authorship, select an appropriate journal for their manuscript, and deal with reviewers' comments.

Oral Communication

> After hearing us emphasize the importance of preparing slides that were readily visible from even the back of an auditorium, two students approached us. "Is what you said about designing slides really correct?" one of them asked. The other then commented, "We were just at an all-day symposium in which you couldn't read even half of the slides!"

Graduate students need to develop their oral communication skills, as a variety of types of presentations will be required of them in their career. Not only may they be called upon to present their research and ideas in seminars to colleagues, but they also need to be able to convey the importance and implications of their work to professionals in other fields, and to lay audiences and policymakers. Moreover, in addition to formal presentations, many informal oral communications are required of successful professionals. The ability to discuss one's work informally with another individual may be even more essential to one's professional success than skill at giving a formal research talk.

Language Skills

> An international student came in one day to say that he had been unable to find one commonly used word in his Russian-English dictionary. The word was *gunnabe,* as in "It's gunnabe difficult to solve this problem."

Oral communication is a particular problem for many students who are not native speakers of English. Frequently, students from outside the United States associate with individuals from their native country while abroad. This is easy to understand—in a foreign land, it is comforting to have the camaraderie of individuals who speak your language and come from the same background. Unfortunately, however, we have actually witnessed students' proficiency in English decline over the course of their studies because they associated almost entirely with individuals from their native land and thus had limited opportunities to practice their English. Therefore, visiting scholars need to make an effort to interact daily with native speakers of English. Being able to speak the language is absolutely essential to receive the most benefit from their training program and the opportunity for networking it affords.

Networking

> "I can't go to the special reception for people interested in wetlands conservation," said a graduate student who was attending his first professional meeting.

"I already promised my labmates that I'd go drinking with them. Besides, I hate going to events where I don't know anyone."

For most students, graduate school represents the first real push to develop their professional network. Certainly the most immediate need students will have for a network comes when they are applying for positions. They will need to have cultivated relationships with faculty who will be able to provide strong letters of recommendation—but the need does not end with the acquisition of employment. Students will also need letters to get promoted, to obtain funding, and so forth. The time to begin developing a network is not at the point one is required to submit letters of recommendation. That is, students should immediately begin to build their network.

Graduate students often do not realize how critical a strong network can be in the development of their career. Even if the importance of networking is brought to their attention, very junior people may think it a rather cynical and distasteful perspective on the realities of professional life. Nevertheless, the need exists, and one of the techniques that students must learn if they are to be successful is the ability to network and to promote themselves. Moreover, a strong network can be one of the joys of professional life: A worldwide network of colleagues can be a source of intellectual and moral support as well as friendship.

Job Skills

Considering a Range of Options

> At the start of our workshops on career planning, we usually ask participants where they hope to be in a few years. The majority of graduate students and postdoctoral fellows at research-oriented universities tell us that they want a tenure-stream faculty position at a similar institution.

Traditionally, most students in doctoral programs set their sights on obtaining a tenure-stream position at a research-oriented university. Despite the decline over the past decades in the availability of such positions (National Academy of Sciences, 1995), many faculty still encourage their students to seek such positions (Zigmond, 1996). Students' desire for such positions may be partially due to limited information about and role models on careers outside of academia. Students need to investigate actively the broad range of positions that are available to them and actively seek role models and mentors outside of academia.

Applying for a Job

> The applicant had no idea how to prepare for a job interview, and it showed. When asked how much space or start-up money he would need, he said that he

had no idea. When asked what salary he would expect, he thought for a while and then replied that his postdoctoral stipend was $21,000 and he would like to make at least that much as an assistant professor.

Students must develop an understanding of how to apply and interview for positions. This means learning how to create a résumé or curriculum vitae (which includes knowing that there is a difference!), write a statement of interests, get letters of recommendation, prepare for interviews, and conduct oneself during an interview. Perhaps one of the most surprising discoveries to students is learning that they should be interviewing their prospective employer as well as being interviewed by them.

Advanced Skills

A research associate submitted his first grant application to the National Institutes of Health. He attached his full curriculum vitae in place of the standard two-page biographical sketch, included a thirty-one page research plan despite the twenty-five page limit, provided no budget justification, and attached the table of contents at the end of the proposal. When it was pointed out that there were hardly any guidelines that he had actually followed, he said: "I never read instructions. And besides, those are just some bureaucrat's recommendations." His application was not funded.

Depending on what position the trainee eventually hopes to obtain, development of certain additional skills may be essential. Students can develop skills in teaching by providing an occasional lecture or running a course at their institution, a community college, or other such venue. Students should invite others to attend their lectures and provide feedback. They also should assemble lecture outlines, syllabi, and teaching evaluations into a portfolio to be used later in their job search. Students also can take part in workshops offered by their local faculty development office.

The development of grant-writing skills can begin upon entry to graduate school. Students may first try their hand at applying for a fellowship. In later years, they might write a research grant or, at the least, assist someone else who is writing such an application.

Supervisory skills can be developed starting with the supervision of a high school or undergraduate student researcher, work-study students, or laboratory aides. It is never too early for students to start mentoring. They can begin by mentoring high school students, undergraduates, or even fellow graduate students.

Responsible Conduct

"Why don't we just send our research article to a couple of journals at the same time?" the student asked. "Then publish it in whichever one accepts it first."

Ethical behavior is essential to the research enterprise, and as a professional in training or in practice, one must adhere to standards for responsible conduct of research. What is ethical is not always obvious, however. Standards of responsible conduct for practitioners in a discipline often derive from a combination of values central to that profession and conventions that that field has adopted. Thus, individuals need to make a concerted effort to determine what the rules are and then to follow them in their daily practice.

Knowledge of what is acceptable conduct is not enough. One must have a system for resolving conflicts that arise when needs or obligations conflict, thus creating an ethical dilemma. In such situations, one frequently must make a hard decision between two or more imperfect solutions. It is essential that students gain practice in making such decisions through the study of cases and discussion of scenarios.

Survival of the Fittest: An Unworthy Approach to Graduate Education

> One faculty member told us, "Spending time on professional development is nothing more than coddling poor students. At my institution we simply place students in a lab, close the door, and see what they're like five years later. The good ones always survive."

Graduate students may not develop a complete set of survival skills. Yet without them, individuals will have difficulty publishing manuscripts, obtaining research grants, or teaching, and therefore they will have difficulty being hired and promoted at most institutions that provide employment to researchers. Consequently, many trainees will be "underemployed" or will leave their field altogether. Some have argued that given the oversupply of Ph.D.s in most areas of research, attrition is not bad, but leads to survival of the fittest. We believe that this reasoning is inaccurate. First, it assumes that those who leave research are less capable of making important contributions than those who remain. Yet there is no reason to believe that a strong correlation exists between intellectual capacity and a native ability to communicate, teach, prepare a curriculum vitae, or formulate a research article. Indeed, much talent is wasted through attrition. Second, high attrition is dispiriting. It reduces the willingness of students to enter training and it reduces the collegiality of those who do. Third, the financial loss resulting from even a small percentage of trainees' dropping out of the system is staggering. For example, we estimate that approximately $250,000 is spent to train each doctoral student in the sciences. Given the current state of federal funding for research and training in the United States, attrition represents a tremendous waste.

Special Populations, Special Concerns

> "If you go ahead with your plans to get married," the student's advisor told her, "it'll take you at least two more years to get your Ph.D. And if you're going to start worrying about your husband's career as well as your own, then you might as well quit now."

Whereas we believe that most survival skills are useful to all professionals, we also postulate that the need for explicit instruction is particularly high for certain groups, including women and minorities in addition to first-generation preprofessionals and older students. Many of these individuals are faced with additional demands, such as the ability to function without an ethnic support group, obtain "knowledge of how to negotiate the academic system" (Etzkowitz, Kemelgor, Neuschatz, and Uzzi, 1992), or obtain access to the informal networks through which much important information is communicated (Hensel, 1991; Olmstead, 1993). These challenges may be partially responsible for demographic disparities such as the great underrepresentation of minorities in graduate training programs and the relative sparsity of women in the higher academic ranks (Etzkowitz, 1992; Zigmond and Spear, 1992). Whereas long-term improvements in the broader social system may be desirable, we must offer these individuals strategies for coping with the present demands of scientific life if we are to increase their participation in all fields of research (Henkart, 1990; Brush, 1991). The survival-of-the-fittest model advocated by some faculty places a disproportionate burden on groups that are underrepresented in a discipline, and thereby postpones the day on which the demographics of that field is comparable to that of society as a whole.

Not only is there a need among special populations for explicit instruction or some other access to information traditionally disseminated through the "old-boys' network," but a need also exists for a forum for discussing concerns unique to special populations. Such issues may include balancing work and family, or dealing with backlash from affirmative action.

The Need: Explicit Instruction in Survival Skills

"Life is less bleak. I am more confident about finding a job. Your workshops gave me tools to improve my chances of succeeding."

Given the significant limitations of traditional mechanisms for acquiring survival skills, we encourage the implementation of programs that provide explicit instruction in these essential abilities. Elements of successful programs frequently include some combination of lectures, discussions, readings, written exercises, and practical experience. At the University of Pittsburgh we offer a series of eight seven-hour workshops, one per month in the fall and spring terms. Each workshop is devoted to providing instruction in a specific survival skill, and instruction in research ethics is an integral part of the program. For example, we discuss issues of honorary authorship, plagiarism, and confidentiality in review in our workshops on writing research articles; and topics such as scholarship, responsible use of time, and integrity in designing graphics in our workshops on oral presentations. These sorts of issues are emphasized throughout the lectures, and over lunch, small groups discuss an ethical dilemma related to the workshop topic.

Our workshops are not designed to develop proficiency in these abilities; to do so requires much effort and practice on the part of the individual. Rather, we aim to provide trainees with an introduction to the essential elements of these skills, and then offer them information on a wealth of resources (on-campus services, print and on-line materials) that they can use in developing proficiency in these skills. What is at least as important, through our workshop we encourage students to take an active role in designing their training program and their future.

These programs ensure that all students receive training in a broad range of survival skills while reducing overlap in faculty effort. Such instruction is costly. It requires both time and money. Yet we believe that part of our professional obligation as trainers of graduate students is to provide instruction in the skills necessary for success in graduate school and beyond.

References

Bird, S. J. "Overlooked Aspects in the Education of Science Professionals: Mentoring, Ethics, and Professional Responsibility." *Journal of Science Education and Technology,* 1994, *3,* 49–55.

Bloom, F. E. "Training Neuroscientists for the 21st Century." *Trends in Neurosciences,* 1992, *15*(10), 383–386.

Brush, S. G. "Women in Science and Engineering." *American Scientist,* 1991, *79,* 404–419.

Etzkowitz, H., Kemelgor, C., Neuschatz, M., and Uzzi, B. "Barriers to Women in Academic Science and Engineering." In W. Pearson, Jr., and I. Fechter (eds.), *Who Will Do Science? Educating the Next Generation.* Baltimore: Johns Hopkins University Press, 1992.

Henkart, M. "Introduction." In *Careers in Biological Sciences: Advancement for Women and Minorities.* Report on the April 1990 Arlie House Workshop, 1990.

Hensel, N. *Realizing Gender Equality in Higher Education: The Need to Integrate Work/Family Issues.* ASHE-ERIC Higher Education Report no. 2. Washington, D.C.: School of Education and Human Development, George Washington University, 1991.

National Academy of Sciences, Committee on Science, Engineering, and Public Policy. *Reshaping the Graduate Education of Scientists and Engineers.* Washington, D.C.: National Academy Press, 1995.

Olmstead, M. A. "Mentoring New Faculty: Advice to Department Chairs." *CSWP (Committee on the Status of Women in Physics) Gazette,* 1993, *13,* 1, 8–11.

Swazey, J. P., Louis, K. S., and Anderson, M. A. "The Ethical Training of Graduate Students Requires Serious and Continuing Attention." *Chronicle of Higher Education,* March 9, 1994, pp. B1–B2.

Varmus, H. Statement on the National Academy of Sciences Report "Reshaping the Graduate Education of Scientists and Engineers" before the Subcommittee in Basic Research, House Committee on Science, July 13, 1995.

Zigmond, M. J. "Helping Our Trainees Find Jobs: The Need for Some New Realities." *Journal of NIH Research,* 1996, *8,* 21–23.

Zigmond, M. J., and Spear, L. P. "Neuroscience Training in the USA and Canada: Observations and Suggestions." *Trends in Neurosciences,* 1992, *15,* 379–383.

BETH A. FISCHER, M. Ed., and MICHAEL J. ZIGMOND, Ph.D., codirect the Survival Skills and Ethics Program at the University of Pittsburgh, Pittsburgh, Pennsylvania. As part of that program, they offer an annual trainer-of-trainers workshop for faculty interested in implementing their model for providing formal instruction in survival skills and ethics. Beth Fischer is an instructor in the Department of Instruction and Learning, and Michael Zigmond is professor of neuroscience, psychiatry, and instruction and learning.

Many graduate students need—and learn to acquire—more mature intellectual perspectives.

Developing Self-Authorship in Graduate School

Marcia B. Baxter Magolda

Adults in contemporary America are expected to be productive citizens who can manage their own affairs. They are expected to make informed decisions for themselves and their fellow citizens, appreciate diverse perspectives, manage conflict appropriately, and act responsibly in their communities. They are expected to be lifelong learners in the face of constant change and increasing complexity. Meeting these expectations requires the ability to develop one's own perspective—the capacity for *self-authorship.*

Self-authorship requires complex assumptions about the nature of knowledge, namely that knowledge is constructed in a context based on relevant evidence, that evaluating evidence is necessary to decide what to believe, and that each individual has the capacity to make such decisions. Furthermore, self-authorship requires a sense of identity through which individuals perceive themselves as capable of knowledge construction. It also requires interdependence with other people to gain access to other perspectives without being consumed by them. As a result, self-authorship is more than a skill; it is a way of making meaning of one's experience.

My longitudinal study of college students' assumptions about knowledge revealed that 2 percent of the seniors and 12 percent of the participants one year after graduation used contextual knowing (Baxter Magolda, 1992). *Contextual knowing* includes viewing knowledge relative to a context, understanding that some knowledge claims are more valid than others, and using informed judgment to determine what to believe. Similar research on reflective judgment showed that college seniors used reasoning characterized by the assumption that knowledge claims are personal opinions, and thus were unable to explain the role of evidence in making interpretations (King and

Kitchener, 1994, p. 167). Graduate students in master's programs and early phases of doctoral work tended to view knowledge contextually and use evidence to interpret, yet did not fully use reflective thinking in which knowledge claims must be evaluated in the context in which they were generated and remain open to reconsideration (King and Kitchener, 1994). Thus self-authorship is rarely fully developed by the senior year and often is still in its early stages in graduate school. Understanding entering graduate students' ways of knowing and teaching in ways that help them learn to author their own knowledge is essential to help them meet expectations held for them as adults in contemporary society.

This chapter explores the graduate experience of sixteen students who were interviewed annually about their learning experiences, their ways of knowing, and their development during graduate school. They are participants in an ongoing longitudinal study that began during their first year of college in 1986. Their stories help educators conceptualize graduate education in ways that promote self-authorship.

The Evolution of Students' Ways of Knowing

I began my longitudinal study of college students' intellectual development in 1986 with 101 first-year students at Miami University. Miami University is a public, four-year institution with a liberal arts focus. In annual interviews I invited students to talk freely about their role as learners, the role of instructors and peers in learning, their perception of evaluation of their work, the nature of knowledge, and educational decision making. These interviews yielded their assumptions about knowledge, and experiences that affected those assumptions throughout their college experience. Eighty students participated through all four years of college.

During college, three ways of knowing were evident in this group. *Absolute knowing,* or the assumption that knowledge is certain and known to authorities, was prevalent in the first two years. *Transitional knowing,* or the assumption that knowledge is partially certain and partially uncertain and known through following a learning process, existed for some students in their first year and was the predominant way of knowing in the remaining three years. Fewer students used *independent knowing,* or the assumption that knowledge is uncertain and everyone has their own biases, during college; this became the prevalent way of knowing during the fifth-year interviews (Baxter Magolda, 1992).

Continuing this study into the years following college graduation made it possible to explore the evolution of assumptions about knowledge in work and advanced educational settings. Seventy participants continued in the postcollege phase of the study. Of that group, only two were members of underrepresented groups. By year eleven, or seven years after graduation for most participants, forty students remained in the project. Their occupational fields include insurance, sales, accounting, computing, teaching, mental health, advertising, communications, business, banking, real estate, retail management, airline services, and government services. Annual interviews in the post-college phase were informal conversational interviews (Patton, 1990) in which participants described important learning experiences in their work, academic, or personal lives, and how these experiences affected their thinking. These sixty- to ninety-minute telephone conversations yielded an ongoing account of participants' ways of knowing during their twenties. (All were traditional-age students in college.)

Sixteen of the postcollege participants entered graduate school: seven immediately after college, eight more in year six, and one in year eleven. Of this group, nine were women, eight attended full-time, and one student entered a doctoral program after completing her master's degree.

The Emergence of Self-Authorship in Graduate School

Rather than recount brief stories of all sixteen graduate students here, I chose to tell three students' stories in some detail to illustrate the difficulty of moving from embracing multiple perspectives to constructing self-authored perspectives. (All research subjects' names have been replaced by pseudonyms throughout this chapter.) Two students, Lowell and Alice, recount graduate experiences that actively promoted their development of self-authorship. A third student, Cara, shares her struggle toward self-authorship in the context of more traditional educational settings. Experiences of other students, including those in professional schools, are available elsewhere (see Baxter Magolda, 1996b).

Exploring Multiple Perspectives. Lowell was already an independent knower on entering his graduate program and thus was amenable to exploring multiple perspectives. Reflecting on his undergraduate experience in our fifth-year interview, he noted that learning had become a process of really trying to think and seriously consider others' points of view. His graduate program furthered his emerging self-authorship through its focus on class discussion of the implications of the readings for national security and evaluation based on that discussion and papers. Lowell perceived this format as "focused on learning." He explained:

> It's the sort of class that builds upon itself, so that every time we talk about something, if you've forgotten what we talked about earlier, then you're going to miss the point. But if you attend class and do the readings, then you're not going to miss it because it doesn't repeat itself but it shows its face in different ways. It is like building a brick wall, you need all of it to make intelligent statements and to think about the things that happen.

Lowell also viewed the short papers as a way to think about the material:

> They all go back to take the basic model or different tools to look at a situation, and compare it to different situations— we talked about the Iran Contra affairs

and the Marines in Lebanon—different issues that have come up in our national security, and can you explain them. You've got the basic tools and you try to manipulate them and see if they work. And if they don't, why, and if they do, why? So you really have to be thinking; you have to be on your toes. So it's not by any means easy.

The basic model and different tools Lowell refers to here form a framework for thinking about issues. Exploring how these models and tools relate to different contexts is the process through which Lowell and his classmates try to make intelligent statements and think about national security issues. This process goes beyond applying a formula to students' forming their own opinions. This is evident from Lowell's description of the teacher and class discussions. Of one professor he said:

> Our professor starts off the class with some anecdote about his experiences, not in a joking manner, just very straightforward. They're often funny, but that initiates discussion. And he sort of acts as referee, and we kind of throw arguments back and forth at each other. He'll summarize things and say "Okay, here's this, this and this," or he'll tell us a fact that he's seen because he's worked so closely with it. And then we discuss it and say, "Ah, well you know, that's wrong," or "they shouldn't have done that." It is a different type of learning.

Lowell's professor initiated the discussion, inserted his perspective in the midst of the students' exploration, and entertained their commentary on his own experience. Debating multiple views was a mainstay of the class discussion. Lowell reported:

> I enjoy taking the argumentative side if there is one; if someone is speaking conservatively, then I take a liberal view. And if the opposite is the case, I take the opposite view. But it's fun; I enjoy, not arguing, but discussing. If they come to arguments, then we've failed. Mulling over an issue or a topic and trying to get all perspectives that are possible—I really enjoy that.

Lowell acknowledged that this discussion led him to debate with himself what to think sometimes:

> . . . especially when people bring up facts that I didn't know. You are going to have a theoretical opinion and that hopefully is based on facts that you have learned. In the Soviet Union class there are a lot of things now that I'm learning that I didn't know and that makes what my answers would be different. So I don't think, I guess, my beliefs or values haven't changed, but if you know something to be a fact and it is different from what you believed, if you don't change, if you are not pragmatic, then you're just going to sink. And if you close your eyes to the truth or what other people see as truth, then you're going to fail. That's when arguments happen [when people don't consider other perspectives].

Lowell's focus in these discussions was to access as many perspectives as possible. He noted that opinions need to be based on facts, yet at the same time stated that closing your eyes to what others see as truth is dangerous. How these experiences in his first year of graduate school affect his learning comes through in his comments on how he approaches learning:

> I am more thoughtful. I guess before it was getting a lot of the facts down. And now it's, like with the national security, you truly try to analyze, try to really think. For example, in my Soviet Union class, we're taking facts that we've hopefully learned and applying them and [are] always open to new facts if we find them. That doesn't mean closing our mind to facts.

At the end of his first year of graduate school, Lowell described himself like this:

> I think I'm more patient. I'm more willing to open myself up to other sorts of experiences, other people's points of view, more open-minded I think. I don't want to give the impression that it's wishy-washy, just more open-minded. I still like, as I say, to discuss. And I do enjoy taking a position and sticking by it or trying to. And perhaps I learn more when I'm forced not to stick by it, hopefully.

Lowell embraced the thinking process emphasized in his classes and embraced trying to merge the facts with others' perspectives. Although he was learning to construct his own perspective, I had the sense that he was focused more on a process for knowing than on committing to a perspective. We explored this idea further during his second year. When asked whether he needed to decide on his own views in his graduate work, Lowell responded:

> Oh, I don't think so. I don't know. Sometimes it's hard to come to a conclusion because there aren't really any good answers. Otherwise we'd be sitting in the White House or in Congress. I think it's good the way it is. I don't think it's bad not to have the answers. It doesn't mean—. If a decision has to be made, you're going to have to make it; if it really, truly has to be made. Someday something will come your way and you'll have more of an opinion about something or a belief that what you now believe is really the truth or whatever. I don't think it has to— you know, there is no one truth. So I don't believe that you have to come to a decision.

Lowell conveyed that decisions are possible, and implied that he might be capable of making them, but he clearly was not pushed to do so in his graduate work. In this same conversation Lowell advanced the notion of acquiring a cohesive view at the end of a course. I asked him to describe how he achieved that view if one does not have to come to a conclusion. He said:

> I think everyone has, especially at our age, their own set of opinions, or beliefs. And in doing the readings, that's a big way of picking up other things to agree

with or refute your own beliefs. In class there's really not time to pull out numbers and so forth to the arguments. But the books provide a wealth of information.... so from the readings and also from the class discussion, listening to
people. You are hopefully going to have people of different opinions so that you
can have a sounding board and they can question you and you can question
them. Through these two routes, it is possible, and I think I will be able to come
up with some better, if not the perfect one, understanding of the topic. I might
change my views; might keep them the same; might make them stronger.

Lowell used the readings either to support or to negate his views; similarly, he used classmates' perspectives to work out his arguments. Knowing that
the "perfect understanding" of the "final view" is not possible, he worked
toward a view he could effectively argue. His graduate program promoted his
self-authorship in terms of engaging him in the process of exploring multiple
perspectives and building arguments, but it did not force him to choose what
to believe. His awareness that decisions would have to be made materialized
in his foreign service work after his graduation. In that work context he was
able to analyze situations, make his own decisions, and stand up for what he
thought was right even in the face of disagreement from his supervisor.

Doing What Feels Best. Alice's master's program in counseling, like
Lowell's program, emphasized multiple perspectives and thinking for oneself.
In contrast to constructing arguments about issues, however, her program
focused on experiencing counseling work as a way to arrive at one's perspective. The experiential emphasis was evident in both classroom and internship
dimensions of Alice's graduate work. She described the majority of her classes
like this:

We did a lot of videotaping and audiotaping that were reviewed with the professor and kind of critiqued, you know, that type of thing, with different counseling styles. And I thought that was real helpful. I guess just memorizing the
concepts and writing them down is one thing, but then practicing them is a
whole different ball game. And it helped me, I think, to find out which styles felt
more natural for me, and it has kind of helped me evolve into what theoretical
background that I kind of adhere most strongly to. Like I said, by the lecture,
"This sounds a little better than this one," but by doing it some of them really
feel better, seem to fit better than others. And the actual doing them on tape
really helped in that process, I think.

The tentativeness in Alice's language—"*kind of* helped me evolve into what
theoretical background that I *kind of* adhere . . . to"—revealed the newness of
thinking for herself. Alice entered graduate school holding some transitional
assumptions about knowledge and looking for information and practical skills
to help her function effectively as a counselor. Her graduate program encouraged her toward self-authorship through the program's focus on developing
one's own theoretical foundation via experience. She explained further how
this took place:

Well, you read all these hundreds of different counseling theories and it's just real overwhelming and confusing. They tell you at these orientation things that they want you to kind of work with it and develop your own—you know, not that you have to pick one theory and say, "I'm this," and never do anything else. But they kind of want you to have in the back of your mind that you should be trying to evolve and select one that you feel is going to work best for you. You know, just try them on and see which ones fit your own personal philosophy and things like that. And by actually doing them and seeing them on tape, that helped me to do that process.

Pressing Alice for how she made such decisions, I received this response:

I guess it just went with my personal philosophy, the way that I kind of view the world anyway or view people anyway. Like I said, it just felt better. I felt like I was able to be more genuine using that group of techniques and that type and style of counseling.

Her faculty openly stated that she should try various approaches and determine which ones fit best for her. They offered opportunities for her to engage in this process and critique the results with them. Her criteria for deciding on a theoretical foundation, however, was limited to what felt natural. Alice's criteria for constructing her own perspective developed further during internship experiences her second year. Describing this work, she offered:

I have a site supervisor who I review all my cases with pretty regularly, a couple of times a week really. And then once a week I'll be driving to meet with my advisor, who will also be supervising me as far as going over my cases as well. So it seems like it's going to be real tight supervision really. I'm glad it is. I would feel like I was floundering without it. It's definitely something that they see as a real important component. They can give me some insights or different strategies that they feel might be effective. And a lot of times what they're doing is just kind of letting me flounder through it and go through the process myself. And while that's hard, it's just like with anything else. I remember it and use it better if it's something that I came up with than if they just told me, "Use this technique; this works best for this."

A subtle shift is apparent in Alice's recounting of her internship; she is coming up with something by going through the process herself and using supervisors' insights as input. The details of how this moved beyond what felt right became more clear as she explained a change in thinking about her counseling work:

The hands-on experience through my practicum and internship has made me realize nobody else is in this room with me when I'm doing this counseling session. And so, for me to be clear on these issues I need to figure them out for myself. Not to say that I'm ever going to figure them out, but to know where I stand on them and to think them through. And I think that's kind of encouraged that process. It's you and your client sitting there. I feel like if I'm not sure where I stand or I'm not clear on what the issues are and what the arguments are both ways and process that myself, then I don't see how I can be of any help at all to this client. So I think that's really encouraged me to do that.

Like Lowell, Alice sees the need to think things through and figure things out for herself, even if a perfect answer is not available. The immediacy of sitting with her clients did prompt her to need to know where she stood. Her responsibility to her clients, even in an internship setting, pushed her to take a stand. Her need for clarity on "what the arguments are both ways" implies that she was moving toward evaluating evidence to decide on her stance. Asked how all this affected her, she said:

> I think that I'm more independent; I'm more of a self-thinker, if that makes sense. I'm questioning things more, and I'm not taking—just because I take notes and then that's the way it is and that's all that's been written and that's law. I'm finding that I'm really questioning things and issues. Like with the dual diagnosis. I'm really sorting stuff out for myself instead of just taking notes about everybody else's opinion. In that way I think I'm a lot different.

Although the conversation did not produce the specific criteria Alice used to "sort stuff out" for herself, it is clear that she was engaged in self-authorship. The experiential component of her program, along with processing that experience with faculty, helped her move in that direction. Alice's professional work after graduating continued to promote her self-authorship. She found herself making decisions about her clients that she felt were right for them given the context, and she acted ethically despite potential risks resulting from disagreements with others.

Struggling Toward Self-Authorship. In some graduate programs self-authorship was not directly encouraged. Cara's master's program in clinical psychology is an example of how difficult achieving self-authorship is when the environment does not support it. Cara was disappointed as she began her work because her peers were very competitive and her classes focused on memorization. She explained:

> I thought [the program] would be a little more intellectual and kind of like group studying and people sharing ideas. It's much more competitive. Everybody wants to get the A. If you know something, you only share it with a few people because you don't want anyone else to do better than you. And everyone's—I guess psychology graduate schools are like this—everybody has the Ph.D. on the brain. You pretty much walk in and you take a lot of notes and you leave. And it's run like a drill sergeant; he's like "We're going to do this, this, and this." It's not how I thought it would be. I thought we'd be more on the same level. In the Ph.D. program at [another school] I know that they're more on the

same—they are treated more adult-like in their classes. And their views are—I mean, they sit around and talk. They study.and learn. I personally learn better when I am able to just understand everything and when I know all the whys in understanding it. This atmosphere is the "what." "Can you memorize everything in your chapters? You don't need to understand it." I don't think that is right at this level. It's like a cow; I'm chewing up information and then spitting it back. That's all I'm doing. But I do know it.

Despite "knowing it," Cara was not sure this knowledge would stick with her. At this point Cara was a transitional knower who wanted to understand instead of memorize. When she did encounter multiple perspectives, her transitional tendency to follow the instructor's lead was reinforced. For example, she described one class like this:

We're learning to do diagnosis. There are so many different perspectives. But we're just following his perspective for the moment. He said, "This is going to be a biased class. You'll think of it in my perspective." I mean, he told us that. He wasn't worried about it. And I have no perspective, so it doesn't bother me.

Because she had no immediate perspective of her own and was not encouraged to construct one, Cara's transitional way of knowing was encouraged.

The lack of stimulation in her program led Cara to take a part-time and eventually a full-time job. She reported that success in her program required minimal work and consequently she felt she learned very little. Her lack of interest resulted in dragging out her thesis for a year. Her thesis was the first component of her program she felt was a useful learning experience, primarily because two of her coworkers were open to talking through her work with her. Although she judged this to be a good learning experience, she told me, "The more I think about it, I have not applied this learning to get ahead." Cara's lack of self-authorship and its de-emphasis in her master's program resulted in her going through the motions without being sure why she wanted this degree. Her reasons for choosing it were to avoid other options that seemed undesirable and to achieve financial benefit and respect. Her two years in a master's program and a thesis had brought her no closer to a self-authored vision of her career goals.

Cara's doctoral work proved to be more encouraging of self-authorship. Cara reported that her classes were seminars in which "we are all on same level of knowledge." Classes focused on reviewing journal articles and discussing them in class. She reported that teachers were not defensive in responding to students' ideas and questions. Despite these dynamics, Cara still struggled in some ways in the seminars due to what she called "lack of social preparation." She described the class atmosphere like this:

Some people like competitiveness to make them work harder—I am mildly competitive, but more into doing for myself. I don't like the feeling—"what did you get?"—not helping each other; that makes me tense, and interferes with my learning. The program is small; that is better for me because I'm not a big speaker in class. I'm more likely here to get involved. The only problem with small is you have to get along—there is nobody else. I am clicking with some, but there are no women [in the program]. In psychology there were a ton of women. I would be more comfortable if there were more women.

Part of Cara's discomfort stemmed from what she viewed as the male students' style in interaction. Her account demonstrates that it was not a knowledge issue. She reported:

Socially I wasn't prepared to be a good interactor in these classes. I knew I was smart enough. Others had no problem; I would wait, didn't want to cut others off, felt unsure, and my thoughts were not completely formulated. Others didn't [hesitate] —men in particular. People said I needed to participate. Ph.D. seminars were totally different than what I had experienced, and I struggled with the lack of direction. It was hard until I got comfortable with people, then I could get in more. I am still less vocal; this has to do with being female. Men cut people off; they don't care. They want to tell what they know. Some are from MBA backgrounds; they are not introspective. I wasn't fitting in with this Ph.D. environment, but was just as knowledgeable; I wasn't expressing it their way. I have made an effort to move toward this. I have tried to change; I noticed I cut people off more; it is not a conscious choice, I just jump in. Before I would have said, "I'm sorry." I don't state the obvious [because] I feel like that is boasting. Why would I tell someone what they already know?

Initially Cara's hesitation stemmed from being unsure of her thoughts and inexperienced in seminar discussion. Yet even when she felt as knowledgeable, she was careful about how she approached others. Cara saw herself as capable of constructing knowledge at this point but did not feel comfortable telling other people what she knew. She acquired some feedback about this issue via a group project. She explained:

I worked with a guy on a project in a statistics course. I had already had a lot of it, and he hadn't. We had a computer project. I knew the package and he wanted to practice. I would say, "Why don't you try this?" the translation being, "This would work." Sometimes he would and sometimes he wouldn't. When it worked, he would act surprised. I said to him that he didn't trust that I knew this. He got upset! He said he couldn't tell from my tone of voice if I knew it. I hadn't thought of it that way. It was eye-opening. Wow! He is one of first people I questioned about it, and he was honest and told me.

Cara discovered that her way of communicating mediated others' perceptions of her knowledge. This occurred in Cara's third year of doctoral work. After five years of graduate study, she was still struggling with the issue of self-authorship. She was disadvantaged in her doctoral seminars by the traditional teaching in her master's program and an environment dominated by students with styles different from hers. The stress of this environment led her to reevaluate her approach. She reported this change:

> I have had a good intuitive sense but have ignored it; like in bad relationships, my stomach would clench. Then I'll have a logic or rational voice saying you are overreacting. In the last six months I've tried to listen more; I spend 20 minutes a day doing breathing exercises. I am used to running around, reading to help myself; read what someone else is saying rather than listening to myself. I started having health problems; the doctor said it is related to emotional issues or stress and anxiety. The more I'm listening to myself, I'm allaying fears. I'm paying more attention to me than other people. I made some bad decisions as a result of listening to others. For example, I changed my major to psychology to stay at home with a boyfriend. I am sick of listening to others!

Cara is beginning to trust herself. Her sense of her own ability to self-author has emerged slowly because of the nature of her experience. Her experience causes me to wonder what would have happened had she attended Alice's master's program instead. That issue is taken up next in the analysis of these students' experiences and principles for promoting self-authorship.

Creating the Conditions for Self-Authorship

The master's programs that Lowell and Alice attended illustrate the characteristics that were common to all but two of the master's programs (Cara's and one MBA program) attended by my sixteen longitudinal participants. Cara's doctoral program also illustrates these same characteristics. These programs create conditions for self-authorship through teachers' assumptions about knowledge, their assumptions about students, and how they act on the two sets of assumptions to create teaching practice. An analysis of these three factors and their effect on students' self-authorship creates a structure for promoting self-authorship in graduate education.

Graduate faculty in these programs conveyed three assumptions about knowledge to their students. These included knowledge as existing in a context, constructed by individuals, from multiple perspectives. Multiple perspectives were introduced and explored in areas ranging from social work issues, counseling theory, and pedagogy to economic theory, business practices, and government policy. Faculty encouraged exploration of these perspectives in various contexts, including one's clients or customers, current economic data, and events around the world. Faculty conveyed, often directly, that students would be responsible for deciding what to believe for themselves.

These assumptions about knowledge were related to faculty members' assumptions about graduate students. With few exceptions, they assumed that graduate students were capable of reading the material in the field of study,

processing its multiple perspectives, thinking about the material for themselves, and developing their own perspective in light of the contexts under
study. This may have been an overestimation of students' ways of knowing at
least upon entrance to graduate school. Because students still held some transitional assumptions and were developing independent assumptions, they were
stronger in exploring ideas than in bringing evidence together to form conclusions. Faculty assumptions did welcome students' independent assumptions, however.

The learning environments students described revealed how faculty
assumptions guided pedagogy. Classes were predominately seminars in which
students were encouraged to process the readings and think about their implications. Faculty welcomed student participation and exchange of ideas among
peers. Faculty participated in discussions but did not dominate them. These
dynamics are similar to those of the community of learners described elsewhere in this volume by Conrad, Duren, and Hayworth. Faculty's simultaneously sharing their expertise and valuing students' perspectives and experience
led students to feel treated as adults in the learning environment. A few students like Andrew in his MBA program and Sandra in her social work program
reported being pushed to defend their positions on various issues (compare
with Conrad, Duren, and Hayworth's critical dialogue notion). The more typical situation was that students were not pushed to use evidence and come to
conclusions, much like Lowell's experience. The push to decide occurred more
readily when students had direct experience as in Alice's internship and in full-
time work settings outside of graduate school. These data are consistent with
Conrad, Duren, and Hayworth's data on the value of powerful professional
development experiences.

These educational practices engaged students' emerging independent
knowing and created conditions for its expansion. Students embraced multiple perspectives and thinking for themselves, even though they were more
enamored with the process than with struggling to make decisions. At the same
time, they did become aware of the central assumptions of contextual knowing, namely using evidence within a context to formulate one's own perspective. Their learning environments more often offered them practice in
exploring perspectives, however, than in evaluating them. Thus students
moved into contextual knowing in terms of understanding that some knowledge claims are better than others, that this judgment depends on evaluation
of evidence in a context (for example, Alice working out her stance), and that
one must support one's judgment by articulating this evidence (for example,
Lowell honing his arguments). Students' ability to act on this way of knowing
remained limited by lack of practice.

The graduate learning environments described here used the three principles for promoting complex ways of knowing that emerged from these students' undergraduate experiences: validating students' ability to know, situating
learning in students' experience, and engaging students in mutually con-

structing meaning (Baxter Magolda, 1992). The first two principles were main-stays of most graduate experiences. More attention to the third, however, would have strengthened students' self-authorship.

Most of these students further developed self-authorship in their work experience after graduate school. Using the ninth- and tenth-year interviews with my longitudinal participants, I identified four dimensions of self-authorship: trusting one's ability to make knowledge claims, establish priorities, and commit to both; the emergence of a solid sense of confidence to direct one's life; learning to balance external forces with one's own perspective and knowledge; and developing an internal identity that supports acting on one's knowledge and priorities (Baxter Magolda, 1996a). Both Lowell and Alice demonstrated growth in these dimensions, primarily from encountering situations in which they had to use their knowledge, take a position, and act on it in their work setting after graduate school.

These students' stories show that many graduate programs do promote self-authorship by respecting students' thinking, engaging students in exploring multiple perspectives, and conveying that students must construct their own perspectives by using the evidence of their discipline. These settings welcomed students' current ways of knowing. Settings that did not welcome students' ways of knowing, such as Cara's master's program and to some extent her peers in her doctoral program, did not promote self-authorship. The stories also convey that more emphasis on how to construct one's perspective, how to balance it with external forces, and experience that strengthens confidence and internal identity is needed. Attention to these components would stretch students' ways of knowing and develop their contextual knowing capacity further. Most graduate faculty hope their classrooms will be consumed by mutual dialogue, exploration of complex ideas, and mastery of the complexity of their discipline. Faculty insight into students' ways of knowing helps create conditions for students to engage in this kind of learning. Conveying the need for self-authorship must be accompanied by learning how to self-author one's perspective during graduate study.

References

Baxter Magolda, M. B. *Knowing and Reasoning in College: Gender-Related Patterns in Students' Intellectual Development.* San Francisco: Jossey-Bass, 1992.

Baxter Magolda, M. B. "Developing Self-Authorship in Young Adult Life." Paper presented at the Association for the Study of Higher Education Conference, Memphis, Tenn., Nov. 2, 1996a.

Baxter Magolda, M. B. "Epistemological Development in Graduate and Professional Education." *Review of Higher Education,* 1996b, *19*(3), 283–304.

Boyer, E. "The Educated Person." In J. A. Beane (ed.), *Toward a Coherent Curriculum.* Alexandria, Va.: Association for Supervision and Curriculum Development, 1995.

Glaser, B., and Strauss, A. *The Discovery of Grounded Theory: Strategies for Qualitative Research.* Chicago: Aldine, 1967.

King, P. M., and Kitchener, K. S. *Developing Reflective Judgment: Understanding and Promoting Intellectual Growth and Critical Thinking in Adolescents and Adults.* San Francisco: Jossey-Bass, 1994.

Patton, M. Q. *Qualitative Evaluation and Research Methods.* Thousand Oaks, Calif.: Sage, 1990.

MARCIA B. BAXTER MAGOLDA is professor of educational leadership at Miami University, Ohio. Her teaching and scholarship focus on epistemological development in college and young adult life.

A graduate student's decision not to continue in an initial program is that student's answer to one or more questions.

Beginning Graduate School: Explaining First-Year Doctoral Attrition

Chris M. Golde

New doctoral students often find the first year of graduate school very stressful. Sometimes they feel stupid and incompetent, believe that their admission was a horrible error, live in poverty, cannot imagine how they will get the reading done, and wonder whether they have not made a terrible mistake. To be sure, most students successfully battle internal demons and external obstacles, and emerge some years later with the Ph.D. in hand. Still, too many students choose to leave their doctoral program by transferring, withdrawing, or completing only a master's degree.[1] Attrition during the first year of graduate school accounts for nearly a third of all doctoral student attrition (Bowen and Rudenstine, 1992; Golde, 1996). Another third drop out before candidacy and a final third postcandidacy, although this varies considerably by department and discipline.

Attrition during the first year, then, is an important window into how things can go wrong for students. Such a "bad beginning" is often explained at the individual level. Either the student did not have "the right stuff" intellectually, emotionally, or temperamentally, or some external event (family, illness) intervened. It is tempting to explain away attrition in this way; not only does it allow for individual variation and nuance, but it removes responsibility for attrition from the institution or the department (Golde, 1996; Lovitts, 1996; Nerad and Miller, 1996). Individual explanations are insufficient, however. To understand doctoral-student attrition, we must critically examine the role of discipline and program in shaping student experiences.

New Directions for Higher Education, no. 101, Spring 1998 © Jossey-Bass Publishers

Socialization in Graduate School

The focus here is on the first year of doctoral education. A common and useful framework for thinking about students' early experiences with the discipline and program is socialization theory (Baird, 1990; Corcoran and Clark, 1984; Egan, 1978; Turner and Thomas, 1992). The socialization process is one in which a newcomer is made a member of a community—in the case of graduate students, the community of an academic department in a particular discipline.[2] The socialization of graduate students is an unusual double socialization. New students are simultaneously directly socialized into the role of graduate student and are given preparatory socialization into a profession. There are four general tasks of transition and initial socialization into graduate student life and the future career common to most doctoral students.

The first task is that of intellectual mastery. The primary mechanism for gaining intellectual competence is through coursework and other intellectual and work settings, such as lab work and field work. The key question students are asking is: "Can I do this?"

The second task is learning about the realities of life as a graduate student. Students often ask themselves whether or not it is worth it to struggle through. The key question at stake is: "Do I want to be a graduate student?" The third task is learning about the profession for which one is preparing. Students are determining whether they are suited to the work, and whether it is the best choice for them to make. The key question students are asking is: "Do I want to do this work?" These two tasks together are how the student determines whether graduate school is an acceptable path, and whether the career she or he is training for is a good alternative. The overarching question students are asking is: "Is this the right choice?"

The fourth task is integrating oneself into the department. Students must determine whether this particular department is a good fit for them. Relationships with faculty, staff, and peers play a critical role here. The key question students are asking is: "Do I belong here?"

Methods

These data come from a larger study on doctoral student attrition (Golde, 1996). In this study I interviewed students who had left four departments at one research university. Two of the departments were in science fields (geology and biology) and two were in the humanities (history and English). These four departments represented a variety of attrition rates and patterns. First-year attrition accounts for about one-third of the overall attrition in three of the four departments.

Overall I interviewed fifty-eight students who had started and then left one of these four Ph.D. programs between 1984 and 1993. All former students were interviewed in 1995–1996 about their experiences during the entire span of their graduate school career. Below I focus on the interviews with the eighteen students who left during the first year of their doctoral program. Of these, eight were women and only one was an international student (Canadian).

The university these students were attending is one of the top twenty-five doctorate-producing universities in the country. It is highly selective in its departments, emphasizing relatively small cohorts of students. The emphasis is on full-time study, and students in most doctoral programs can reasonably expect to receive their tuition and a modest stipend for at least four years of study.

Common Reason for Leaving

One reason was expressed commonly by the leavers in all four of the departments.[3] This was the dawning realization that the life of a graduate student, which could encompass the next half-dozen years of their life, and the life of a young faculty member were characterized by a single-mindedness of purpose and an all-consuming lifestyle that they did not want to embrace. One student summarized this dilemma by analyzing the trade-offs:

> I knew that it was going to be five to seven years, but it hadn't really hit me that in order to be five to seven years on campus here doing this, it means that you're not somewhere else doing something else.[4]

In short, several students realized that they preferred to live a life that was broader and more balanced. The academic life was an enticing one, but the trade-off of focus and commitment of time would be substantial. In several cases, family commitments were crucial in making this decision. As one man in biology said:

> [When] I had set my goals, I didn't think I'd ever be married, let alone have kids. So spending the next ten years of my life trying to get a job basically—that was ok. But then when I started thinking about bringing a wife through it and bringing a family through it, it was real hard.

These students have taken a hard look at the second question—"Is this the right choice?"—and answered "no." They reached the conclusion that the academic lifestyle, both as a student and as a professional, are predicated on an unbalanced lifestyle that they were not willing to lead.

Reasons for Departure of Science Students

Doctoral education in the sciences differs dramatically from study in the humanities. In general, science students spend several undergraduate semesters and summers apprenticing in the practice of research science. Biology students, for example, work as undergraduate research assistants in the laboratories of faculty members. Geology students attend summer field schools, often as a requirement for their undergraduate degree. Once enrolled, a science graduate student must connect with a faculty member, an advisor who serves as their primary mentor and educator. Science graduate education is closely linked with the research enterprise, particularly as funded by industry and government. For most science graduate students, funding of tuition and research costs, selection and execution of research topic, and mentoring through graduate school are all dependent on successful incorporation into the research team of a faculty advisor in their research role as principal investigator on a grant. It is critical for a student to make this connection quickly, usually during the first year. Consequently, students have ample opportunity for mentorship, but also experience significant dependencies.

Three reasons for attrition in the first year of graduate school emerged as common themes in the accounts of the eight attrited science students I interviewed: the decision that a particular department was the wrong place to study and the subsequent decision to transfer, concerns about the job market, and advisor mismatch.

Wrong Department. Half of the science students I interviewed reached the conclusion over the course of their first year that the particular department in which they were studying was not a good home for them. In each case the student decided that he or she was unhappy with the advisor he or she had selected or with the research opportunities available. Each of them then investigated other options and transferred to another graduate department in the same field. Subsequently, they reported being significantly more personally and intellectually satisfied; they had either finished or anticipated finishing their degree.

These science students are negatively answering the third question—"Do I belong here?"—while simultaneously answering "yes" to the other questions. Nerad and Miller (1996) also report these as problems in the early years, calling these students "institution switchers."

Job Market. Several of the students also commented on the job market, which played a role in their decision making. In one case the student was aiming for an industrial career. He was uncertain whether a master's or Ph.D. degree would serve him better, and quite quickly he decided to stop with the master's degree. Another student came to realize that the job market in his particular subfield was very saturated; there would not be any faculty retirements for the foreseeable future. This was one of several reasons he decided to leave the Ph.D. program. For the science students I spoke with, the job market was an important factor that helped inform their answer to the question, "Do I want to do this work?"

Advisor Mismatch. Two students described personality clashes with their advisor. Both of these students selected their advisor without having worked with them in advance, and one did so despite the advice of other students. One said:

> I talked to some grad students at the time, and I did hear from some of them that many students had problems getting on with [this professor], and I did not heed that warning as much as perhaps I should have.

Both of these students had difficult relationships with their advisor, marked by dissimilar working style and the inability to communicate. The other explained:

> Sometimes it seemed like he was being malicious on purpose. And the other student of his felt like that, as well. I didn't want to admit it at first. . . . That's

mostly the reason why I left [the University] because I felt my self-confidence eroding at every second, and I knew that if I didn't leave there that I would drop out of graduate school and never go back.

Neither of these students wanted to abandon their studies, and so each of them transferred to another institution. They both selected their new institution based on a strong affinity for their new advisor, and in each case, personality was as important as scientific acumen. The first continued his account, describing talking with the professor who would become his advisor at a conference.

Here I suddenly got exposed to the alternative that I had turned down the previous year, which was going to work with [a particular professor at another university]. It just reminded me, meeting him in person, of what a nice guy he was. I suddenly realized how important that was to me because at the time I was intensely not liking [the professor with whom I was working].

Again, these science students are answering the "Do I belong here?" question. The prompt for the question is a problem with the advising relationship.

Reasons for Departure of Humanities Students

Humanities graduate programs differ significantly from those of the science fields. Most humanities graduate students major in their field as undergraduates and write a senior thesis, thus immersing themselves in a small piece of research and writing. The early years of graduate training feature much more emphasis on coursework as the primary site of learning, as contrasted with learning in the process of conducting research in science labs. Most of the humanities students at this university do not serve as research assistants to faculty members; instead they apprentice as classroom teachers by spending several terms working as teaching assistants. Building a relationship with a particular faculty member is less important across the board than in the sciences; some students make such a connection, others build a team of advisors for the dissertation.

Three reasons for attrition in the first year of graduate school were common in the accounts of the ten humanities students I interviewed: intellectual difficulty, practice of the discipline did not meet expectations, and the faculty life did not meet expectations.

Intellectual Reasons. Several of the humanities students indicated an intellectual component to their attrition decision. Several of the students found that the graduate study of a humanities subject differed significantly from undergraduate study. Rather than learning content, they were expected to master theory and method. Several reported that they were not adept at making this transition, nor had they realized that this is what would be expected of them. As this historian reported:

I love being told a story. [But] the books that we were reading seemed so trivial sometimes, and I never saw the points being made. I would sit in class, and we would go over these books, and people would come out with these points that the author had made, and I would be astounded. . . . I was reading it to learn the history, and that's not what graduate school is about. You're not supposed to be learning content anymore. You're supposed to know all the content. You're supposed to be learning theory, and I'm not really geared toward that.

These students found that they were not skillful at the kinds of learning and theory extension expected in graduate humanities. These students answered the "Can I do this?" question negatively.

Practice of Discipline Did Not Meet Expectations. Some students found that when they became graduate students they were exposed to the full-time practice of the discipline in a way in which they had not been exposed as undergraduates. This exposure revealed that they were not as suited to this life as they had assumed. A former history student realized that the practice of history involved a lonely tedium he could not endure.

I really began to have questions as to whether I really wanted to do research for the rest of my life. In history it is a very isolating kind of work to be doing. Most of my friends, both undergraduate and in graduate school, were in the sciences, and they would work with their professor on a project and work with other students in the lab, so they would not be focusing only on their own work. I really began to find that wearing after a while, just showing up at the library, being the only one working on my project, having relatively little human interaction as a necessary part of the job. It just began to grind on me that day after day after day, it's the same thing. The basic process is "Well, today I'm getting up and I'm going to the library and I'm doing research and I'm going to do some writing. And what am I going to do tomorrow? Well, the same." It's the same basic process over and over again and after a year of doing that it just got to the point where I couldn't imagine doing forty years of that.

An English student described the differences she found between undergraduate education, which focused on the texts and the canon, and graduate training, which emphasized a philosophical and analytic perspective.

I found myself really frustrated by the tendency for everybody to kind of factionalize within the department in terms of their perspective on English and American Literature. You know, it was either you were a feminist, or you were a deconstructionist. It just drove me nuts. And you'd go into these small classes and everybody would be arguing their point of view and were kind of militant about it and nobody wanted to talk about the text. I was coming straight from undergrad where pretty much that's all you do—talk about the text—it was really a shock to me.

These students realized that they were neither suited to humanities graduate school nor the professional life. Their first year of graduate school provided a good look at the life, and they answered the "Is it the right choice?" question with a "no."

Reality of Faculty Life Did Not Meet Expectations. Students also reported having their expectations about the faculty life dashed. Many became history students because they desired to emulate the faculty members who had excited them about the study of history. They wanted to become great teachers and interest others as they had had their interest kindled. Instead, they learned that research was the important emphasis in faculty lives, a value that was communicated to graduate students. Students were advised not to put too much time into their teaching, nor to expect that teaching would be central in their future lives as faculty. Whereas first-year scientists answered the "Do I want to do this work?" question in part by referencing the job market, first-year humanities students focused on the texture and quality of faculty life.

Importance of Program Detail

The details of the curricular structures and other mechanisms for integrating students into the department affect how easily students make the transition into graduate school and which kinds of problems contribute to attrition.

Biology Versus Geology. Departments have different strategies for the organization of the first year of graduate school. Within the two science departments, two advisor selection strategies are at work. In the geology department and some parts of the biology department, students match with an advisor at admission. Usually students meet the faculty member when visiting campus or at professional conferences. Students select an advisor based primarily on their scientific reputation. By contrast, in some subfields of the biology department, students participate in "rotations," a year-long program in which they spend ten weeks each in a few different labs, working on small projects, and getting to know the culture of the lab as well as the science. Consequently, those students who participate in rotations are less likely to find advisor mismatch to be a problem that led to attrition.

Another key issue for some of the geology students was that they had an opportunity to work, or maintain work relationships, at a large, publicly funded research facility near campus. As a result, these students reported that they did not make close connections on campus. Their primary affiliation remained at work, rather than at school. The inability to become integrated into the campus community became a central factor in these students' drifting away from their doctoral program. This outcome reinforces the importance of full-time enrollment and immersion into the culture of the graduate department. It also highlights the role of student choices: In these cases, the department clearly encouraged the students to focus on their school-based relationships, advice the students ignored.

Third, the geology department facilitates transfer between the master's degree track and the Ph.D. track. The geology master's degree takes two to three years to complete. Master's students take the same courses, are linked into research projects like their doctoral colleagues, and have access to several years of financial support. To many students, it is difficult to distinguish master's students from doctoral students. Indeed, the Graduate Student Handbook devotes several pages to detailing the processes for making the switch from one track to the other. As a result, geology students who wish to stop their education and enter industry jobs are able to complete a master's degree. Students I interviewed who felt discouraged had a viable option, and many took advantage of it.

The biology department takes a different approach. The master's degree program is a year-long course-based program. Students in the doctoral program rarely meet master's students, who are unfunded and do not participate in research projects. Biology students who feel discouraged do not have an easy path into a master's program that provides them a valuable set of skills. Ironically, the ease of program transfer may have exacerbated the overall attrition rate in geology relative to biology.

English Versus History. Within the humanities departments, there is a significant difference in the coursework structures for the first year. In history, students participate in a year-long "core" of courses, which includes a term-long research paper writing requirement. In the process of this intensive research and writing, students get a taste of the nitty-gritty aspects of conducting historical research on primary sources. By contrast, English department students spend the first year taking courses that are structured in the same term-length format as undergraduate courses. Thus, history students are more quickly immersed in the discipline and exposed to dissertation-type work and faculty work. This leads, I believe, to the much higher levels of first-year attrition in the history department, relative to the English department, which has almost no first-year attrition.

The differing cultures of the departments regarding graduate student teaching also surfaced. The English department has far more intensive pedagogical instruction and apprenticeship. This has the benefit of integrating the teaching and research functions more closely and mitigating the frustration that several history graduate students related regarding the undervaluing of teaching. On the other hand, these teaching experiences serve to delay the formulation of a dissertation topic and dissertation-level research and writing. Consequently, the kinds of frustration and difficulty with research and writing reported by historians turned up much later in the accounts of English department students.

Conclusions

Although some of the reasons students give for leaving a doctoral program are personal, and hence unaddressable by the department, these data suggest that many disciplinary norms and departmental structures can affect the attrition decision. The small sample size represented here means that these findings should not be considered absolutes, but rather give researchers and those interested in assessing and reforming graduate programs some recommendations of fruitful lines of inquiry.

Though leaving graduate school certainly suggests that the students did not have a good beginning, I concur with those who argue that early attrition is vastly superior to late attrition (for example, Bowen and Rudenstine, 1992). The amount of time and money invested in a year of graduate school might be thought of as an investment in a student's future by learning whether the life of graduate student and training in academic research is really a sound choice.

Indeed, many of the interviewed students in the study did not feel regret at having started and then leaving graduate school. Many listed a variety of positive gains from being at this university. Some simply enjoyed the overall experience, others recalled the people they had a chance to meet and the skills they learned. Learning how to teach and how to think analytically are two examples of generalizable skills.

Another reason students gave for not having regrets was that they had explored the option of graduate school, and learned that they were not suited to it. They were able to lay to rest the "road not taken" questions.

> I'm very glad to have gone and spent the year doing it because otherwise ten years from now if I hadn't gone to graduate school, I'd probably want to know, "Would I really have been happier being a history professor?" And now I know that it's not really for me in the long run.

It was predominantly those who transferred who expressed regret. In these cases, the time spent at this university felt like a wrong turn and a waste of time.

By suggesting that there are positive aspects to first-year attrition, I do not want to suggest that universities are not responsible for structuring their admissions and program requirements in a way to maximize the opportunity for student success. Conceptualizing the first year of graduate school as a socialization process into a discipline and graduate student life may be a useful tool for assessing and improving departmental practices. Although a potentially daunting political challenge, such a review might serve many departments and students well.

To move one step further, these data allow us to challenge notions of good and bad beginnings and attrition. Rather than locating "goodness" or "badness" solely in outcomes—persistence versus attrition—it might be useful to assess the authenticity of the socialization experience.

A good first-year graduate school experience might well be one in which a student is deliberately exposed to the practice of the life they are being prepared to enter (as in the long research paper requirement in the history department), opportunities to observe the lived life of professional practitioners (as in the biology rotation), and opportunities to interact with graduate students at various stages of the process to learn about graduate student life (as in geology lab group assignments). While these experiences might result in some attrition, I would argue that structuring experiences in order to help students answer all four of the socialization questions during the first year is in the best interest of all concerned.

"Good" beginnings, then, help students to make informed, early decisions in response to the socialization challenges they face. "Bad" beginnings delay students' ability to answer key questions or provide experiences that inaccurately reflect student and professional life.

Notes

1. The most extreme expressions of stress are murder of faculty (Burd, 1996), depression, and suicide (Lovitts, 1996).

2. I use the term *discipline* to refer to the field of study. I use the term *department* to refer to the organizational unit dedicated to the study of a particular discipline on a specific campus.

3. I use the term *leaver* to denote a student who left their program permanently. This does not carry the pejorative weight of *dropout,* and can be contrasted with *persisters* and *completers.*

4. All quotations have been edited for grammatical flow and readability. Ellipses have not been included, except when considerable editing was done.

References

Baird, L. L. "The Melancholy of Anatomy: The Personal and Professional Development of Graduate and Professional School Students." In J. C. Smart (ed.), *Higher Education: Handbook of Theory and Research.* New York: Agathon Press, 1990.

Bowen, W. G., and Rudenstine, N. L. *In Pursuit of the Ph.D.* Princeton, N.J.: Princeton University Press, 1992.

Burd, S. "Murder of Three Professors at a Thesis Defense Stuns Campus." *Chronicle of Higher Education,* Sept. 6, 1996, p. A14.

Corcoran, M., and Clark, S. M. "Professional Socialization and Contemporary Career Attitudes of Three Faculty Generations." *Research in Higher Education,* 1984, 20(2), 131–153.

Egan, J. M. "Graduate School and the Self: A Theoretical View of Some Negative Effects of Professional Socialization." *Teaching Sociology,* 1978, 17(April), 200–208.

Golde, C. M. "How Departmental Contextual Factors Shape Doctoral Student Attrition." Doctoral dissertation, Stanford University, 1996.

Lovitts, B. "Leaving the Ivory Tower: A Sociological Analysis of the Causes of Departure from Doctoral Study." Doctoral dissertation, University of Maryland, 1996.

Nerad, M., and Miller, D. S. "Increasing Student Retention in Graduate and Professional Programs." In J. G. Haworth (ed.), *Assessing Graduate and Professional Education: Current Realities, Future Prospects.* San Francisco: Jossey-Bass, 1996.

Turner, C.S.V., and Thomas, J. R. "Socialization Experiences of Minority and Majority Women Doctoral Students: Implications for Faculty Recruitment and Retention." Paper presented at the meeting of the American Educational Research Association, San Francisco, April 1992.

CHRIS M. GOLDE is assistant professor of educational administration at the University of Wisconsin–Madison.

The master's degree is much underestimated as a contributor to effective careers.

Students' Perspectives on Their Master's Degree Experiences: Disturbing the Conventional Wisdom

Clifton F. Conrad, Katherine M. Duren,
Jennifer Grant Haworth

Caught between the Ph.D. degree and the baccalaureate degree, master's degrees have long been viewed in the higher education literature as "second-class," a "credential," a "steppingstone" to the Ph.D. and, perhaps worst of all, a "consolation prize" for those not allowed to pursue the doctorate. Such a negative portrayal of master's programs is reflected in the voices of policymakers, administrators, and faculty as well as in national reports, studies, and scholarly papers (Glazer, 1986; Green, 1987; Pelczar and Frances, 1984; Stewart and Spille, 1988). To wit, the senior academic officer (Barak, 1987, p. 32) of a statewide governing agency has suggested that the "master's degree remains the weakest collegiate degree in America. . . . If there is a skeleton in higher education's closet, surely it is the poor quality of master's degrees that have been consistently neglected over the years."

From our perspective, the literature on master's degree programs suffers from two limitations. One, there is almost no literature on how students experience their master's programs, much less the effects of their experiences on students themselves. Two, the literature does not draw on students' perspectives: It is anchored mostly in the voices of faculty and administrators—nearly all of whom have been associated with graduate programs in the liberal arts and sciences at research universities. Conspicuously missing are the voices of students and program graduates, especially those representing professional fields of study such as business and education, which altogether enroll more than 90 percent of all master's students.

NEW DIRECTIONS FOR HIGHER EDUCATION, no. 101, Spring 1998 © Jossey-Bass Publishers

In light of these limitations and the compelling need for a national study of master's programs, we—including our colleagues—conducted a major study of master's programs in this country. Altogether, we interviewed nearly 800 faculty, administrators, employers, students, and alumni associated with forty-seven master's programs representing eleven fields of study ranging from engineering and business to applied anthropology and microbiology. Drawing on this comprehensive database, which we have used to sketch a national portrait of master's education and to advance a theory of program quality, we recently reanalyzed the student and alumni interviews from our study (184 students and 147 program graduates) in light of this question: How do students interpret and evaluate their master's experiences, including their impact on themselves and others (see Conrad, Haworth, and Millar, 1993; Haworth and Conrad, 1997). In this chapter we report our findings and conclusions.

On the basis of what interviewees communicated to us about their overall master's experiences, we found that the majority of students and program graduates viewed their experiences in a much different light than that of conventional wisdom.[1] In broad strokes, interviewees characterized their master's degree experiences as highly beneficial as learning experiences, as professional development experiences, and as leadership experiences. In exploring each of these three venues, we discuss the character and enriching features of students' experiences as well as the effects or outcomes on students.

A Meaningful Learning Experience

Contrary to the conventional wisdom, students across our forty-seven–program sample communicated to us in many different ways that they found their master's program to be meaningful. While there were many enriching features of their programs—such as a master's thesis or project and faculty mentoring—two features, which we labeled *community of learners* and *critical dialogue,* emerged as signature aspects of their learning experiences.

Community of Learners. Particularly in master's programs that were not ancillary to the doctorate as in some of the doctoral-granting universities we visited, we found that a *community of learners* was a centerpiece of students' learning experiences. When students and program alumni elaborated on what they meant by *community,* they emphasized the collegial and collaborative relationships among faculty and students; more often than not, they said that faculty and students learned from one another as "co-learners." In some programs, faculty invited students to work with them on research projects and to coauthor papers and, in so doing, de-emphasized traditional faculty-student hierarchies by viewing students as valuable sources of knowledge and understanding. Many students and alumni described the collaborative teaching and learning that took place in such programs, as illustrated by a nursing alumna who told us about the colearner roles that professors and students took on in one of her courses:

Once a week we would assemble for a [clinical] seminar—where everyone would gather together and discuss patients and different styles of handling things. But, you know, we really didn't even need a faculty member there. Students would get up and make a presentation on this or that—we pretty much ran the seminar ourselves. Sure, the faculty member would ask a question here or there, but you never felt like you were on the spot and you were up there and people were going to try and humiliate you. It wasn't like that at all. It was very collegial.

In other programs we visited, students stressed a larger "community of learners" and the salience of supportive and caring relationships among faculty, administrators, and students both in and outside of classes, as well as within faculty and student subcultures. Two students in a master's program in environmental studies described the "sense of community" they experienced in this way:

> The program is hard, it's rigorous, but there is a sense of community that holds us together so we can get through it. There is more camaraderie . . . and this is important. It's not like regular programs where graduate students don't know what the others are doing.

Of all the students and alumni we interviewed, few were as articulate in describing a "community of learners" as an alumnus of a master's program in English:

> What makes [this program] happen isn't just the professors, or the quality of the students, or what happens in the classrooms. It's this sense of us as a community, bonded together and tied into this thing that [this program] epitomizes for us. . . . It's a psychological landscape, it's a sense of identity, of belonging to this project. . . . What I'm suggesting is that not only is it a nice perk when it happens, but that it may well be integral to creating the dynamic. It's like a synergy that happens. It's because of this notion that we learn together. I'm not just learning in my class—there is an intensive interaction because of that. It happens at meals, it's just always happening. . . . Intense interactions are typical, never stop around here. That's part of what makes this place work. And it would suggest to me that that's what would energize a graduate community at any university. But it means you have to pay a lot of attention to things outside of the curriculum, and the quality of the professors, and the academic demands that you make on your students. You have to look at the students as a whole, and at their life together. That's what helps create an academic community.

Critical Dialogue. Another feature of students' experiences, one which works hand-in-hand with the concept of a community of learners, is *critical dialogue*. As we came to understand it, this takes place when faculty and students conjointly question existing knowledge, challenge key assumptions in their field, and develop and critically refine new understandings of knowledge and professional practice. In short, critical dialogue is anchored in a two-way, interactive, or *dialogical* (Conrad, Haworth, and Millar, 1993) approach to teaching and learning in which students share and test their ideas along with faculty. A business student described his master's experience as "a conversation" in which faculty encouraged him to "participate in the management of his own education."

Again and again, students and alumni told us that critical dialogues provided much of the fuel for their learning because they demanded rigor and discipline that were not distinctive features of traditional didactic pedagogies. An environmental studies alumnus, for example, discussed the "constant questioning" he engaged in with his peers and professors and then said: "[This program] doesn't make it easy—[as though] this is going to be the right answer. You're constantly asked: 'What is your bottom line, what are your limits, what are your values, what are you making your choices on?' It was not an easy road."

Moreover, many students told us that frequent dialogical interactions—usually originated by faculty but often initiated by students as well—helped them develop critically informed perspectives on knowledge and practice in their field. As one student put it:

> Here the concept of discourse community tends to be very, very strong. People want to hear what other people have to say. As far as the books, you're going to get basically the same books no matter where you are . . . [that's] fairly consistent. What isn't consistent is the people. And the whole concept of critical study of literature has to revolve around this concept of discourse. People talking about why a certain author is great. What is so good about this. Or why they feel someone is horrendous and shouldn't be in the canon. . . . And that has been my experience in all of my education here. I learned far more about these ideas in my classes than I learned from reading Shakespeare by myself.

Effects on Students. When students were engaged as active partners in cultivating collegial relationships and building communal learning environments through dialogical relationships, there were many positive student outcomes. To begin with, such programs enriched students' communication and teamwork skills and, more broadly, helped them develop a better appreciation and respect for collaborative approaches to inquiry, problem solving, and leadership. A theater alumna told us: "When you get ten minds together it can make an incredibly exciting production. And the production teams here— being able to work on them and being a student observing them—just gave you incredible insight. . . . The atmosphere was electric."

Programs that emphasized critical dialogue also tended to have other major effects on students: critical dialogue was instrumental in helping students to become more holistic, critical, and discriminating thinkers and problem solvers. A graduate of an applied anthropology program, for example, stressed that interactions with other students and faculty significantly helped to develop critical thinking:

I learned how to step out of my value system—and that's really hard. That takes time. I remember I started to get so mad at everyone around me because I kept seeing how locked in they were by their own assumptions. . . . You would think you'd get this thinking process in your bachelor's [program], but you don't. . . . It's a whole different experience at the master's level. You learn how to look at yourself and different cultures in a more critical way. You just don't go along with the flow; you just don't accept everything that everyone says and does any-more. You really get critical. You really begin to question.

A nursing graduate told us that she credited the critical dialogue in her master's program with "transforming" the way she approached her professional practice. In her words: "Before I was just a robot, I was a good staff nurse. But it wasn't like anything I can do now. Everything now has to be questioned. [During my master's] I began looking through a different lens."

In short, we learned that, more often than not, students had meaning-filled learning experiences during their master's program. In programs fueled by a learning community and critical dialogue in particular, students enhanced their communication and teamwork skills along with their critical thinking skills. They also became more critical questioners of knowledge who had learned to take inquisitive stances toward extant knowledge and professional practice. And for a surprising number of students, the master's experience was a "rite of passage" in which they were transformed. As a graduate of a microbi-ology program put it: "I approach problems differently; I realize there's not always one right answer. I now question more. I see how things relate. I realize that everything isn't just black and white. . . . There's a big difference in me."

A Powerful Professional Development Experience

Labeled by many observers as a "credential" bereft of much substance, one of the major surprises in our examination of student voices was the barrenness of that label. We found, contrary to the conventional wisdom, that the major-ity of students view their master's experiences as powerful professional devel-opment experiences—especially students in professional fields such as business, education, nursing, and engineering. There were, we learned, a number of fea-tures of students' master's experiences that contributed to this interpretation—including critical dialogue and master's projects. Foremost among them, though, were what we label *doing-centered learning* and *integrative learning*.

Doing-Centered Learning. From many students we found that *doing-centered learning* was an important part of their master's experience. As we came to understand it, this meant that students actively and consciously practiced their profession—or craft—through engaging in hands-on teaching and learn-ing experiences. They did so both on and off-campus. As to the former, stu-dents often engaged in doing-centered learning in the laboratory or onstage rather than in the classroom. For example, theater students engaged in the "real work" of staging theatrical productions, microbiology students engaged in "doing science" in the laboratory, and education students participated in "teaching students" in on-campus programs such as Upward Bound.

Without diminishing the enthusiasm that many students had for doing-centered learning on campus, it was their elaboration of the concept in off-campus settings that drew most of their attention and excitement. Specifically, they referred to what we call *professional residencies,* such as internships in government agencies, businesses, and human service organizations for students in fields such as applied anthropology, business, and environmental studies; residencies in theater companies for students seeking careers in the dramatic arts; and practica for students seeking professional advancement in nursing and education. In broad strokes, professional residencies were aimed at challenging students to build bridges between what they learned in class and the "real world" and, in so doing, to develop deeper and more connected understandings of their profession. In most of these residencies, students were given significant responsibilities; in many, site supervisors and faculty provided them with regular guidance and feedback.

Time and again, students told us how much they valued applying and testing their classroom-based understanding of knowledge and practice in real-world professional settings—as illustrated in the voices of graduates of three applied anthropology programs we studied. One student, for example, told us about how her internship in Washington, D.C. gave her a form for "testing and revising" her "academic" understandings of policy development and decision making. Another alumnus said that his practicum had given him new insights into the daily realities of urban planning. In his words:

> The practicum, to me, was the strongest piece because you're out there in the real world. You act in a real-world setting. That's critical. . . . You're only getting half the story sitting here [at the university] learning about whatever it is you're learning about, because implementing it in the real world is a whole other ball game. There's not a textbook out there about what to do about the feud between the social workers and the planners. There's not a textbook about why the grants come down the way they do, how to handle competition, how to become competitive in your grant writing. To learn about competition, personalities, state and local government, institutions, who the players are—all those are things that you can only learn when you're in the practicum.

Integrative Learning Experiences. A second feature that greatly enriched students' professional experiences was what we called *integrative learning experiences.* In a nutshell, this refers to learning experiences that invite connections between theory and practice and, as such, it draws much of its sustenance from doing-centered learning. As we came to understand it, integrative learning experiences include classroom instruction that gives students more than "textbook" understandings of knowledge; faculty modeling; hands-on learning activities such as role-plays, case studies, simulations, field trips, and artistic performances; and bringing nonuniversity workplace professionals into classes.

In the majority of programs we studied, faculty connected theoretical and applied knowledge to real-world problems. To illustrate, a student in a microbiology program told us that not only did the professor lecture on the immunological characteristics of AIDS, but he also invited several AIDS patients to discuss the disease in his class. As this student told us: "It wasn't just textbook and it wasn't just 'here, you have an assignment to do.' It was real. You could talk to these people and see what the disease did to them mentally and physically."

Faculty used a broad range of hands-on learning activities to bring theory together with practice. In an education program, master's students played "educational games" that helped students learn and apply theoretical principles from environmental science. In a business program, students often participated in case studies. As described by a student in the program:

> When I have to go out and actually collect financial indicators from my own work setting or for a case study, I really feel like I'm being bumped up to another level of education. It's no longer hypothetical; it's real-world stuff. In this program, somewhere along the line, after faculty make you learn the theory, they then make you deal with the realistic, and that moves you up to a different level of thinking. That's what I enjoy.

Effects on Students. Especially when students were involved in programs that embraced doing-centered learning—notably through professional residencies—and integrative learning experiences, there were many positive outcomes on students. Among others, students nearly always enhanced their future job possibilities and professional competency. Beyond these, three major sets of positive student outcomes stand out. For one, residency experiences greatly enhanced students' professional identities. An alumna of a nursing program made this point:

> [When I was a staff nurse] you just kind of did what everybody does all the time. That was one of the reasons why I liked my clinical experience so much. Yes, it was hard, but it was refreshing. I remember thinking: "Wow, finally we can think and we can experience things differently." See, since nursing is such a new field, I think this has forced nurses with advanced degrees to have to do more thinking on our feet—reflecting—thinking about how we interface with the other professions, who we are in relation to other professions. We have had to do that because we're still so undefined in terms of how others see us. And since I was new to that, I was still undefined prior to my clinical experience. Now I would know what to say and how to do things. But then [before my clinical practicum] I was still struggling with the idea that nursing was more than just following doctor's orders.

For another, integrative learning activities in particular helped students to develop more holistic, "big picture" perspectives on problems and issues in their field. To give but one illustration, a graduate of a microbiology program told us that, though securing a "credential" to maintain a position in an academic laboratory was the original purpose for beginning a master's program, there was "a big difference in [the student's] contributions at work during the course of [the] master's experience": "Things began to fall together for me. I began to integrate things, to see the big picture. I began to hold my head up in the scientific community. . . . I began to see myself as a scientist who could contribute to the field. . . . And, really, that's the bottom line." Like the majority of students we interviewed, this student found that both doing-centered learning and integrative learning experiences were pivotal in enriching the master's experience in general and professional development experiences in particular.

A Valuable Leadership Experience: Profession and Society

The literature on master's education is virtually silent about master's education and leadership development. To the contrary, we learned that most master's students had a valuable leadership experience that was at once built on the aforementioned features of master's programs and two additional features: a risk-taking environment and cooperative peer learning.

Risk-Taking Environment. Many master's students told us that, in contrast to their undergraduate experience, faculty encouraged risk-taking in their program in order to encourage students to press the boundaries of their own potential and to appreciate the valuable role that risk-taking—and its by-products, success and failure—played in their learning. Faculty encouraged risk-taking in several major ways. For one, they developed and nurtured a "culture"—one anchored in a delicate balance between challenge and support—that encouraged students to explore new ideas and continually test their skills. Faculty provided students with opportunities to discuss their ideas in open forums, examine diverse viewpoints, experiment with new approaches, and learn from their mistakes within a learning context unfettered by undue competition, ridicule, or penalty. For another, many faculty also took risks and, in so doing, encouraged students to do likewise. For example, faculty members in a theater program we visited were directly involved in local theater productions, thereby taking "risks" themselves.

Many students emphasized to us the kinds of trusting, supportive, and challenging learning environments that encouraged them to take risks. More often than not, they referred to faculty who not only pushed them but were there to lend a discerning ear, a critical eye, a helping hand. A theater graduate described the supportive—and challenging—learning environment in her program and emphasized that the program challenged her "to take risks and to trust" herself. Similarly, a microbiology student described how faculty pushed her to move away from "cookbook" approaches toward thinking for herself. Like many students we interviewed, she said that the transition from "dependent" to "independent" scientist was "scary" at first but the process had helped her really "think" like a microbiologist. A student in a theater program told us in no uncertain terms what risk-taking meant to her:

Students are encouraged to do a lot of that around here—to take risks and try out new things. That's been really valuable for me. I've tried risky things, and I've failed, but it was in failing that I discovered my own voice and the impact I can have on an audience. I actually found my edge by going beyond it. I believe that an actress must dare herself to fail; otherwise, she will just fit into someone else's mold instead of creating her own mold.

Cooperative Peer Learning. A second, perhaps more important, feature of students' master's experiences—not least in relation to providing enriching leadership experiences—was cooperative peer learning. In program after program, students and program graduates told us about both their in-class and out-of-class experiences that involved teaching and learning from one another.

In many programs, students were required to participate in various collaborative learning activities—from research teams and study groups to group projects and presentations. Again and again, students told us that, as they worked through group assignments, puzzled through difficult problems in the laboratory, or worked together to mount theater productions, they began to place increased value on what they could learn from their peers. Two master's students in microbiology told us about the collaborative spirit that animated their program:

I learn a great deal from the other students. No one is afraid to talk about their research, and nobody's going to stab me in the back if they find out what I'm doing. Yeah, it's really different than when I was at [another university]. There students didn't enter each other's labs—everyone wanted to keep their work top-secret, and there was a lot of sabotage—ugly things like unplugging people's refrigerators, even in the cancer center.

Throughout our study, students and program graduates told us about the various ways in which they benefited from one another's teaching and learning—from enhancing their teamwork and teaching skills to their ability to learn with and from others. For example, referring to the study group of which he was a part, a business student said: "I've found that 90 percent of the exchange in the program is with other students. The raw brainpower is great. . . . These people bring so many perspectives and ways of thinking. The work is so much better. It's an excellent way to learn."

In many programs, students took the initiative in promoting cooperative peer learning. While there were significant differences across programs in terms of how peer learning found expression, interviewees told us about everything from informal exchanging of ideas over an Internet users' network to journal clubs to brown bag lunches and student-led seminars and colloquia. One student, for example, told us about the dialogue that took place among students at parties:

> I remember sitting at one of our student-organized social events and listening to my peers. The first-year students were so black and white—they thought that all foresters did was pillage the land—and they were heavy into the conservation movement. Then I would listen to how the second-year students talked to them. They provided a broader view on things—they were more informed and less orthodox in their approaches. They spoke with a more holistic perspective on things. And I think that's where a lot of the real learning happened for us—in those informal discussions we had with each other.

A microbiology student echoed this view that much of the "real learning" in her master's program happened in outside-of-class collaborative activities. She told us that her weekly journal club had "forced" her to "become a good speaker." In her words: "You present at least once or twice and we interact. . . . Speaking skills are very, very important. Presenting in the journal club has really helped me with that." Emphasizing more informal activities, a nursing student told us that her collaborative experiences with other students over lunch and after class convinced her that "collegial interactions" produced a "better" and "more professional" nursing practice. "Because of those experiences," she said, "I now use a more collaborative approach at work."

Effects on Students. In our examination of student voices, perhaps the most surprising overall finding was the impact of master's programs on the leadership development of students. In broad strokes, we learned that not only did many master's students become leaders in their profession but, in many instances, they made important leadership contributions to society as well. Though anchored in virtually all of the features of master's programs outlined in this chapter, this finding was especially grounded in the two features discussed immediately above.

In a very real sense, we found that many master's students went on to become the real leaders—the "movers and shakers"—in their respective professions. Although this capacity for leadership was fostered in the "expert training" they received in their master's program, the "risk-taking" and "cooperative peer learning" were often what enabled program graduates to become more than technical experts. Again and again, interviewees told us that taking risks and learning from and with their peers helped them develop into more imaginative, resourceful, and self-confident professionals who had not only the tools but the "qualities-of-mind" that helped them to become leaders in their profession. More broadly, students' collaborative learning experiences provided much of the foundation for providing leadership in their profession through sharpening their interpersonal, communication, teamwork, and "joint problem-solving" skills—skills widely considered essential to providing leadership.

Moreover—perhaps the biggest surprise of all—interviewees told us that their master's experiences inspired their interest in serving as leaders in their communities. An alumnus, for example, said that during his master's program he began to feel "a real dedication to give something back [to the surrounding community]: . . . That became more focused for me during my master's [studies]. . . . The master's taught me how to become actively involved, and I learned how to play this out. Before maybe I was just a good neighbor, as opposed to being a community servant." In a similar vein, a nursing alumna said that during her master's she began to "think that [nurses] help the community through education, support, listening to families and patients, and nobody else is going to do that. Nurses are the leaders in community health support." This message, a message of leadership in the ability and willingness of master's graduates to apply their expertise to community leadership, was echoed throughout our interviews.

Based on our findings, what advice might we give to faculty and administrators who are responsible for designing and administering master's programs? We offer three suggestions. First, since the master's is the terminal degree for nearly 90 percent of its recipients, we recommend that faculty and administrators give serious consideration to designing bona fide master's programs that serve distinctive professional and educational purposes. As we have documented in this chapter, when faculty and administrators view and treat the master's as an important and legitimate degree (rather than as a "consolation prize" to the doctorate), students are far more likely to have meaningful educational experiences that challenge them to develop as leaders in their chosen profession. Second, we urge faculty and administrators to consider incorporating the voices of students and alumni more regularly into ongoing, formative reviews of their programs. As we learned throughout our study, these stakeholders often have keen insights into how various curricular, pedagogical, and programmatic features affect—both positively and negatively—students and their learning. Such insights could be invaluable to faculty and administrators as they seek to understand, identify, and strengthen those learning experiences within their programs that positively enhance students' growth and development. Finally, we believe that faculty and administrators would do well to pay as much attention to culture and pedagogy as they do to curricular content when making decisions about learning experiences in master's programs. In our experience, discussions of program culture (for example, *community of learners, risk-taking environment*) and pedagogy (*doing-centered learning* and *cooperative peer learning*) have seldom been important considerations in the design and administration of graduate programs. Our research indicates that these oft-neglected topics are every bit as important as curricular content and, indeed, may significantly enrich students' learning of the subject matter at hand.

Building Bridges Between Higher Education and Society

At the turn of the century, William James opined that the "Ph.D. Octopus"— the reification of the Ph.D. as the only bona fide degree—was already beginning to dominate higher education in this country. From the standpoint of the millennium, James's prescience runs like a purple thread throughout the conventional academic wisdom and the literature on graduate education. More often than not, the master's degree continues to be characterized as an impoverished relative of the doctorate and unmistakably "second-class." Yet, in drawing on the experiences of those mostly directly involved in master's programs—over three hundred students and program alumni—we learned that students' experiences are anything but impoverished and that, in many instances, they are a "rite of passage" for students.

We conclude that master's degrees should no longer be regarded as second-class or merely credentials or steppingstones to the doctorate but, instead, as enriching and valuable experiences in their own right—especially for the 90 percent of the students who are in professional fields and leave academe after completing their master's degree. By providing students with the kinds of learning experiences, professional development experiences, and leadership experiences that enhance their ability and willingness to become leaders in their profession and in society, master's programs have become bridges between our colleges and universities and the larger society, thereby benefiting not only individuals but society as well.

Note

1. To be sure, there were some noteworthy exceptions. For example, many students in programs in which faculty viewed the master's degree primarily as a way station to the doctorate—or a consolation prize—were unenthusiastic about their master's experiences (see Conrad, Haworth, and Millar, 1993).

References

Barak, R. J. "Skeleton in Higher Education's Closest." In J. L. Green (ed.), *The Master's Degree: Jack of All Trades.* Denver: State Higher Education Executive Officers, 1987.

Conrad, C. F., Haworth, J. G., and Millar, S. M. *A Silent Success: Master's Education in the United States.* Baltimore: Johns Hopkins University Press, 1993.

Glazer, J. S. *The Master's Degree: Tradition, Diversity, Innovation.* ASHE-ERIC Higher Education Research Report no. 6. Washington, D.C.: Association for the Study of Higher Education, 1986.

Green, J. L. (ed.). *The Master's Degree: Jack of All Trades.* Denver: State Higher Education Executive Officers, 1987.

Haworth, J. G., and Conrad, C. F. *Emblems of Quality: Creating and Sustaining High-Quality Academic Programs.* Needham Heights, Mass.: Allyn & Bacon, 1997.

Pelczar, M. J., Jr., and Frances, C. "Graduate Education: Past Performance and Future Direction." In M. J. Pelczar, Jr., and L. C. Solmon (eds.), *Keeping Graduate Programs Responsive to National Needs.* New Directions for Higher Education, no. 46. San Francisco: Jossey-Bass, 1984.

Stewart, D. W., and Spille, H. A. *Diploma Mills: Degrees of Fraud.* New York: American Council on Education and Macmillan, 1988.

CLIFTON F. CONRAD *is professor of higher education at the University of Wisconsin–Madison.*

KATHERINE M. DUREN *is director of continuing legal education for the State Bar of Wisconsin.*

JENNIFER GRANT HAWORTH *is assistant professor of higher education at Loyola University Chicago.*

What happens when we really prepare graduate students to become college professors?

Preparing College Faculty

Jerry G. Gaff, Anne S. Pruitt-Logan

Let's face it. We have never really prepared graduate students to become college professors. Traditional doctoral study is designed to give graduate students the capacity to conduct original research. This is a necessary but insufficient condition for faculty success. After all, most faculty members manage a wide range of roles. Most teach and advise undergraduates, and many also teach graduate students. Many graduate students, however, acquire no experience in the complex tasks of teaching: determining proper goals for student learning; designing courses, selecting learning materials, making assignments, and assessing the achievement of those goals; understanding and working effectively with diverse students; giving academic and career advice; and constructing and assessing curricula in the department. Too many of those who do serve as teaching assistants are given only minor assignments and receive little or no orientation and mentoring to master these tasks.

Faculty members also are expected to provide service to the department, institution, and wider community, but graduate programs are typically silent about this entire range of professional roles. Faculty members, after decades of struggle with the state, church, and administrations, now enjoy authority over the instructional program and the right to participate in the shared governance of colleges and universities. But where do faculty learn to design the curriculum as a whole? Where do they learn to determine who is qualified to teach a subject? Further, where do they learn about the complexities of running modern academic institutions—strategic planning, student and faculty recruitment, financial aid, fundraising, budgeting, and the like—in order to knowledgeably contribute to shared governance? The traditions of academic freedom and tenure are central to the profession, but where do we teach what these mean? Where do future faculty learn about the idea and practice of liberal education?

Another part of the need for new approaches to graduate preparation is that doctoral study is primarily conducted in the small number of specialized institutions that are known as research universities. In fact, 102 universities produce 80 percent of all doctorates awarded in the United States according to the Council of Graduate Schools. Many of these graduates take positions in approximately 3,500 institutions, most of which have very different missions, values, cultures, and conceptions of faculty roles and responsibilities from those in research universities. Too often, the graduate faculties are unaware of the values of different types of academic institutions, and, occasionally, are even hostile to the very places their students will seek jobs. In sum, graduate education is typically disconnected from the realities of the majority of jobs available to new faculty.

Preparing Future Faculty Programs

Programs to prepare future faculty are emerging to correct these problems. They are a recent initiative to provide graduate students opportunities for developing capacities in research, teaching, and service so that, as new faculty members, they can enter the profession as competent professionals who have already begun the process of growth in each of these dimensions.

Many individual universities have developed their own versions of these new programs, and several organizations have launched their own initiatives, usually involving multiple institutions. They include

- Preparing Graduate Students for the Professional Responsibilities of College Teachers by the then-Association of American Colleges
- Preparing Future Faculty conducted by the Council of Independent Colleges
- Future Professoriate Project of Syracuse University
- Compacts for Faculty Diversity operated by the New England Board of Higher Education, Southern Regional Education Board, and Western Interstate Commission for Higher Education
- Preparing Future Professors: A New York State Consortium Project, a collaboration of Cornell, New York, and Syracuse Universities and the SUNY Universities at Binghamton and Stony Brook

These programs have all been supported by The Pew Charitable Trusts or the federal Fund for the Improvement of Postsecondary Education.

Perhaps the most ambitious effort to change the "culture of preparation" is the Preparing Future Faculty (PFF) program, a joint effort by the Association of American Colleges and Universities (AAC&U) and Council of Graduate Schools (CGS) supported by The Pew Charitable Trusts. Launched in 1993, the first phase of PFF awarded grants to seventeen clusters of institutions to develop model programs for incorporating research, teaching, and service components. Although the grants were awarded to graduate schools, each university was charged to assemble a cluster of diverse institutions that represent the variety of American colleges and universities. This arrangement brings the "consumers" of Ph.D.s together with the "producers" to collaborate and determine what qualities are desired in new faculty. It also provides opportunities for graduate students to have direct and personal experience as junior faculty colleagues at very different academic settings. The partner institutions—liberal arts colleges, comprehensive institutions, community colleges, women's colleges, historically black colleges and universities—work together to allow graduate students to explore faculty life in their very different environments.

Clusters were encouraged to develop their own programs based on their own interests, needs, and opportunities, but they were urged to plan their programs in terms of their students' maturity and stage of development, include mentoring in teaching and other aspects of professional development, provide direct personal experience with diverse kinds of institutions, and emphasize emerging and future expectations of faculty. Although programs differ, all incorporate a broader vision of graduate preparation than is usual and provide students with experience in institutions markedly different from their own graduate university.

A second phase of PFF was launched in 1997. The purpose of this phase is to work to institutionalize the best features of PFF programs and to disseminate the lessons learned so as to propagate faculty preparation programs in other settings. Following is a list of the fifteen doctoral-granting universities selected from national competitions—ten from the first group and five others from among the universities that had developed their own PFF-like programs:

Arizona State University
Duke University
Florida State University
Howard University
Indiana University
Marquette University and University of Wisconsin–Milwaukee
Northwestern University
Syracuse University
University of Cincinnati
University of Colorado–Boulder
University of Kentucky
University of Minnesota
University of Nebraska–Lincoln
University of New Hampshire
University of Washington

Including the partners, a total of 108 institutions are included in the second-phase program.

Surveys of Participants

Two coordinated surveys of participants at institutions in the PFF program—only one specific type of faculty preparation program—were conducted during spring 1995 and again in spring 1996. The purpose was to learn about the experiences of individuals involved in these programs. Doctoral students, faculty members at both the graduate university and partner institutions, and administrators at the various institutions were queried.

A set of questionnaires prepared centrally was designed to capture the experiences and views of individuals in the different PFF programs. An advisory committee of experts in survey research was assembled to review the instruments and to give advice about procedures. The process of data collection was decentralized. Questionnaires were distributed to those participants most involved in the programs, as defined by coordinators at each cluster of institutions. Completed forms typically were returned to cluster coordinators, who sent them to the national office; a few were sent directly to the national office, where they were analyzed.

In 1995, completed questionnaires were received from 186 graduate students from fourteen of the seventeen clusters. In 1996, completed forms were received from 171 graduate students, 141 faculty members, and sixteen administrators in fourteen clusters. The results are generally similar, so our primary focus here is on the 1996 survey, with occasional comparison to the earlier one when it amplifies the meaning of the findings.

Because of the decentralized way in which the forms were collected, it is not possible to identify a precise response rate. To the best of our knowledge, 79 percent of the graduate students responded to the first survey, but we cannot be certain enough to venture a specific percentage of the other groups. Suffice it to say that we have 706 reports—378 in the first and 328 in the second study—which is a large but not necessarily representative sample. In year two, a third of the students had been involved two years. Thus it can be assumed that a portion of this group may have completed the first survey as well.

Graduate Student Experiences

The students in 1996 were distributed across the academic disciplines: 29 in English, 23 in other humanities fields, 37 in natural sciences, 44 in social sciences, 16 in mathematics, and 22 in education and other professional fields. Slightly more than half were women; more than half the women were single; nearly two-thirds of the men were married. The average age was 32; 90 percent said they were within two years of finishing their degree; and nearly nine in ten had served as teaching assistants. In both years, more than three-quarters were white and the rest were ethnic minorities, of which African Americans were the largest group.

We asked about the motives that led students to the PFF program. The most frequently checked items were to learn about faculty roles (78 percent), explore interest in being a professor (76 percent), enhance prospects for an academic job (66 percent), improve their teaching (62 percent), learn about other kinds of institutions (62 percent), and intellectual curiosity (61 percent).

The students in both years reported that they had participated in a variety of PFF activities. The two most common involvements, cited by 71 percent, were having visited or worked at a partner institution and attending a series of workshops or seminars on teaching or professional development. Other frequent experiences included working with a mentor at a partner institution (45 percent) and teaching an entire course (34 percent) or a unit (29 percent) with supervision. In these respects they differed little from the earlier respondents.

Whatever their expectations and experiences, the graduate students were impressed with their various PFF programs, so much so that all but three of the 357 respondents in the two years said that they would recommend their program to other students. Although roughly a third expressed some reservation, two-thirds said they would recommend their PFF program without reservation. This global endorsement of quite different operational programs suggests that any such effort to inform graduate students about the realities of faculty life is welcomed, but it gives little guidance to academic leaders seeking to identify which programmatic features are most and least powerful.

We asked what specific benefits they derived. The two benefits reported by more than four out of five were understanding of faculty roles and awareness of diverse institutions. Over three of five reported greater interest in an academic career, ability to compete in the job market, and knowledge about the job search process. The only other item checked by the majority was knowledge about teaching.

People whose judgment is important to graduate students, by and large, support their involvement in PFF. About nine of ten students said they were encouraged by their department head (92 percent) and other graduate students (88 percent). Faculty members at partner institutions were supportive in all but one case. On the other hand, a small minority—less than 20 percent—reported that their major advisor and other faculty in their department discouraged their involvement. These mixed messages received by the graduate students suggest that further work might address ways to secure greater graduate faculty support for faculty preparation programs. In each case the percentages of individuals discouraging these students are slightly higher in the first year than the second, suggesting a growing acceptance of faculty preparation programs by the graduate faculty.

We explored the difficulties students encountered in their PFF programs and found that time was the major concern. Most students had to incorporate PFF activities into already heavy schedules; in general, the PFF programs were add-ons rather than part of a reconfigured course of study. Consistent with one of the major areas of discouragement, students indicated that another of their greatest difficulties was the lack of advisor and departmental support. Given that visitation at partner institutions is a core concept, it is not surprising that arranging transportation also created a problem. When recommending their faculty preparation program to other students, some said they would advise them to carefully consider the time demands and the appropriateness for students at different levels of doctoral study.

A related concern about a faculty preparation program is that it might increase the amount of time students spend in earning their degree. More than four out of five of the students said that participation in the PFF program had little or no impact on their time to degree, and a small fraction even said involvement had speeded up completion, perhaps because they were more motivated to move into an academic career. It should be noted that some PFF programs feature substantial involvement in a number of activities, while others require more limited or focused involvement. These different types of programs might be expected to have a differential impact on time to degree.

One consequence of involvement in a faculty preparation program is that students become more aware of the diversity of institutions and may broaden the range of their career options. In the first survey we asked students about the kind of institution in which they hoped to find employment for their first job: 45 percent indicated a liberal arts college, 21 percent a research university, and 16 percent a comprehensive university. In the second survey we asked how attractive they regarded a position in various types of institutions, so that students rated each type: 71 percent of the respondents found a liberal arts college "very much" attractive, as did 67 percent a comprehensive institution, and 52 percent a research university. It appears that PFF legitimates graduate students exploring work in places other than research universities.

This dynamic is most apparent in the responses to working in a community college, which traditionally has been looked down on by graduate faculty. When asked to indicate in which kind of institution they wanted to find their first job, only 4 percent checked a community college; but when asked to rate the attractiveness of each kind of institution in the second survey, 16 percent checked "very much" for a community college, 44 percent said "moderately," and 40 percent cited "very little." Although community colleges ranked the lowest of these types, they are still at least a moderately acceptable alternative among the majority. At least two explanations may account for these results. First, the negative stereotypes about community colleges that graduate students tend to hold are moderated when students encounter faculty members who are outstanding teachers, thoroughly professional, and may still manage to publish. Second, students are very much aware of the dismal academic job market in most fields, and they are making realistic assessments about where they might locate an acceptable faculty position.

It was anticipated that experience in a faculty preparation program would be valued by hiring institutions, so in the second year students who had been involved in academic searches were asked to tell us about these experiences. Fifty-two had been in a search and 79 percent indicated that PFF had been very or moderately useful. Student comments indicated that they felt clearer about the positions for which they were applying and were better able to develop appropriate cover letters, curriculum vitae, and professional portfolios. Most said that those who were conducting the searches seemed impressed that they had been involved in a faculty preparation experience.

Voices of Graduate Students

Apart from the surveys, graduate students have had many opportunities to comment on their experiences in the PFF program. A student wrote in an essay reflecting on his experience:

> My experience with the PFF project has been one of the highlights—if not the high-light—of my doctoral study. . . . To be honest, I was a little uncertain of how the experience would pan out, considering my status as an advanced doctoral candidate finishing my dissertation. I expected that I would be hearing a number of things I had already heard while at [this institution]. What I soon learned, however, was that [this institution's] mission was not the mission of many other colleges and universities. In the end, I believe that it was my participation in the PFF project that was the key factor in my being offered a tenure track assistant professor position.

Another student, writing about her "capstone experience," said PFF "has been, without question, one of the most meaningful parts of my graduate school experience." In her conclusion, she wrote:

> The first test of the value of PFF was my successful job search. . . . I am convinced that our seminars, the participation phase experiences, interaction with fellows from other disciplines, and interaction with faculty from all types of institutions, has helped prepare me for life in academia.

Another graduate student said that, as a panelist at a conference, "I don't feel like a student. I feel like a professional pursuing a career."

In addition to the above random comments, we might look at comments from graduate students across a variety of disciplines at a single university:

> It was great being mentored—you get so much out of the program when you are closely involved with someone at another institution. You learn about the school, what it's like to teach there, and you get to know the faculty.

> I have heard insights from faculty at other institutions, who are perhaps more likely to have experimented with alternative teaching techniques, such as the use of computers in the classroom or calculus reform projects.

> I feel that I am gaining twenty steps on some of my departmental colleagues who are not benefiting from this program.

> PFF has provided a foundational and life-changing experience. The program supplied a provocative forum for intellectual growth and critical reflection on our system of higher education and graduate training along with crucial discussions of balancing and integrating teaching, research, and service.

> PFF has convinced me of the need to formulate some professional goals before
> I suddenly find myself interviewing for a job.

> I have discovered that there are different pleasures and compromises associated
> with each academic institution. The key is knowing what the pleasures are and
> what compromises will be required to participate successfully in the culture of
> a particular college or university.

Other evidence comes from Duke University, which had participated in the forerunner to the PFF program. Leigh DeNeef (1996), associate dean of the graduate school, reports that he tracked seventy-six graduate students over five years, and of the approximately half that graduated, virtually all found an academic position. Nine were in research universities, sixteen in liberal arts colleges, and nine in comprehensive universities. He drew three major lessons from the two faculty preparation programs he directed: (1) Despite fears from some faculty members, these programs do not "corrupt" students; (2) the programs "guard (students) against too narrow a set of intellectual and research interests" and "keep them competitive for the full range of academic employment;" and (3) the graduate faculty have little experience with the realities of the job market at other types of institutions. He concludes that "Successfully preparing future faculty for a complex and difficult job market is simply not something that any single institution—and certainly not any single faculty mentor—can do alone."

Syracuse University, too, operated its own faculty preparation program before it was selected to become part of the specific PFF program (Tice, Gaff, and Pruitt-Logan, in press). Telephone interviews with more that 70 alumni who had participated revealed that over 90 percent had secured academic employment in the type of position they were seeking. Virtually every person said they believed that involvement in the program was helpful in securing their position. That helps to explain why the Future Professoriate budget has been supported by the university since 1995. It currently has about two hundred graduate teaching associates, a step appointment above teaching assistants, and two hundred faculty members have received special training to be teaching mentors. It also helps explain why the recipients of fully funded graduate fellowships demanded not to be relieved of responsibilities like these, as has been traditional, but to become part of the Future Professoriate program and the enrichment that it provides.

A final perspective comes from the graduate experience of a single student, a case study. Tina Evans (1997) is assistant professor of political science at Bethune-Cookman College. While a doctoral student at Howard University, she was selected for the first cohort of PFF students. She participated in a variety of campus events, including a workshop on Preparing Performance Objectives and a panel on Ethical Issues in Graduate Education; she taught a course on American National Government; she participated in a workshop on Instructional Strategies for Students with Disabilities and a workshop on University Teaching Across Cultural Lines; she was coordinator, moderator, and panelist on a conference on Race, IQ, and Public Policy: the Bell Curve; she met with visitors from the PFF national office, and participated in a workshop on Successful Career Paths in Higher Education and a workshop on Mentoring Graduate students for Faculty Careers.

At partner institutions she did the following: videotaped a lecture at Marymount University, taught a course on American Government at Marymount, participated in a workshop on Preparing for Testing at Catholic University, videotaped a lecture and panel at Bowie State University, team taught a course on Black Politics at Bowie State, attended a faculty meeting at Marymount University and a department meeting at Bowie State, was a panelist on Minority Health Issues at Bowie State, attended University College of Excellence Pilot Advisory Council at Bowie State, and made site visits to Catholic University, Howard County Community College, Bowie State University, and Marymount University.

In addition, she made presentations on The Professional Apprenticeship at the Fifth Annual Conference on the Education and Employment of Graduate Teaching Assistantships and on Lessons Learned and Next Steps for the Preparing Future Faculty Program at the Association of American Colleges and Universities Annual Meeting. Dr. Evans (1997) summarized what she gained from this experience at the latter event:

1. Development of a professional teaching and research portfolio.
2. "I was able to expand my professional network."
3. "I have been able to develop an excellent rapport with students," have "high academic standards that forced (students) to work hard," and receive very good student evaluations.
4. Having been exposed to many aspects of a professor's life, "I have been able to successfully balance responsibilities that I have to the Faculty Association (at Bethune-Cookman) with my teaching and research."

Obviously, not all students involved in faculty preparation programs are successful in a difficult job market; more is involved in whatever success they have than participation in such a program; and these programs are about a lot more than getting a job. Nonetheless, the evidence is growing— from surveys, anecdotes, campus experience, and individual case studies— that faculty preparation programs equip students to become more sophisticated about faculty life in different institutions.

Other Strategic Benefits

People everywhere tell us that PFF "is the right thing to do." But there is more to it than that. We have learned that PFF also offers strategic benefits to departments and universities. In regard to admissions, a faculty preparation program is an excellent way to recruit talented graduate students. The national PFF office has received telephone calls from prospective students interested in which graduate universities offer faculty preparation programs. We are aware of only one university, Howard, that is actively using PFF as an admissions tool, but it has the potential elsewhere.

Retention appears to be enhanced by participation in a faculty preparation program. We know that at the undergraduate level, retention of students is determined to a great extent by the degree of academic involvement. Faculty preparation programs are inherently highly involving experiences, and this may help explain the anecdotal evidence that they improve doctoral student retention. To the extent that students remain in the program, the cost of a degree is reduced, thus producing important financial benefits, as well. As mentioned above, the job search is aided by the faculty preparation experience as well.

All of these assertions about admissions, retention, reduced cost to degree, and the job search need further empirical study, but we believe that such hypotheses can be confirmed. When combined with the reports that faculty preparation programs provide a powerful learning experience—frequently said to be one of the most important of the graduate years—the evidence for overall benefits is significant.

Conclusion and Policy Implications

Obviously, we have much more to learn about faculty preparation programs. Even the oldest has been in operation for only a few years. We know too little about the differential impacts of their various components. Nonetheless, we have made sufficient progress to issue two challenges to traditional forms of graduate preparation: First, all graduate students considering an academic career should have access to a faculty preparation program. Second, all graduate departments and universities that offer doctoral degrees should operate faculty preparation programs. Based on what we know now, for doctoral programs not to operate faculty preparation programs borders on professional irresponsibility.

References

DeNeef, A. L. *The Lessons of PFF Concerning the Job Market.* Washington, D.C.: Association of American Colleges and Universities and Council of Graduate Schools, 1996.

Evans, T. "Preparing Future Faculty: Lessons Learned and Next Steps." Presentation at annual meeting of the Association of American Colleges and Universities, Atlanta, Jan. 1997.

Tice, S. L., Gaff, J. G., and Pruitt-Logan, A. S. "Preparing Future Faculty Programs: Beyond TA Development." In *The Professional Development of Graduate Teaching Assistants.* Boston: Anker, in press.

JERRY G. GAFF is vice president, Association of American Colleges and Universities. He is primarily responsible for the Preparing Future Faculty program and also directs the Network for Academic Renewal, which offers a series of working conferences on topics such as what works in general education, diversity and learning, and internationalizing the curriculum.

ANNE S. PRUITT-LOGAN is a scholar in residence with the Council of Graduate Schools.

Best practices for integrating first-year students into graduate programs include an approach that fosters collegiality and mentoring, based on program structure.

Best Practices for Enculturation: Collegiality, Mentoring, and Structure

Peg Boyle, Bob Boice

American doctoral programs remain the premier training ground for the world's future scientists and scholars (Clark, 1995). Every year, thousands of students enter graduate school with hopes of bright careers; many aspire toward careers as professors and scientists (Boyle, 1996). All of these prospective scholars must begin as first-year graduate students. These students go through a *cultural learning* or enculturation process in which they learn to act as productive members of their graduate department (Corcoran and Clark, 1984). Organizational influences, embodied by procedures and practices, may either facilitate or hinder the enculturation process (Van Maanen and Schein, 1979).

Based on our empirical examinations of graduate education and our knowledge of the graduate education literature, we highlight the best practices for facilitating enculturation. When we examined exemplary departments, particularly their organizational cultures and program structures, we found that exemplary departments distinguished themselves in three ways: They foster collegiality among the first-year students; they support both mentoring and collegial, professional relationships between the first-year students and faculty; and they provide the first-year students with a clear sense of the program structure and faculty expectations.

We begin with a brief description of the study from which our data are taken. We then examine how the research on graduate education corresponds to the best practices we identified.

Methods

Department Effectiveness Ratings. To identify exemplary departments, we relied on the National Research Council (1995; NRC) effectiveness ratings. The NRC periodically rates doctoral programs' effectiveness in training research scholars and scientists on a scale from 0 (not effective) to 5 (extremely effective). The effectiveness ratings of the departments included in this study had a mean of 3.17 and a standard deviation of .44.

Participants. We interviewed sixty-six students and faculty from a large, public research university. We interviewed thirty-six domestic first-year students from ten graduate departments. From each of these ten departments, we interviewed one graduate director and two advanced graduate students for a total of thirty interviews with senior department members. The ten departments represented departments across the physical/life sciences, social sciences, and humanities.

Interview Procedures. The first-year graduate students were interviewed three times during their first year: within the first few weeks of entry, near the end of their first semester, and during their second semester of graduate school. The interviews covered a range of topics. We report the data that relate to their perceptions of the departmental cultures into which they had entered, the social and professional relationships they were forming, and the first-year requirements. Each interview took approximately one hour.

At the completion of the thirty-six new graduate students' first year, we interviewed the directors and advanced graduate students from the ten departments. The directors and advanced students answered questions regarding issues pertinent to the early experiences of graduate students; specifically, departmental policies, practices, and program requirements. These interviews typically lasted approximately one hour. (For the full interview protocols, see Boyle, 1996.)

Best Practices for Enculturating Graduate Students

The exemplary graduate departments we studied shared some common elements: They fostered a sense of collegiality among the incoming students, nurtured the formation of mentoring relationships between the students and faculty, and provided program structure to help coach students toward their primary role as research scientists and scholars. First, however, these departments welcomed their students with a structured orientation that complemented the university-wide orientation.

Orientation. At this large, public research university, campus-wide orientations are held for graduate students. The departments that excel at enculturating graduate students supplement the general orientation with a departmentally sponsored orientation. These departments realize that it is the departmental culture, not necessarily the university culture, to which their incoming students will need to adjust. The graduate directors are very clear about their purposes for sponsoring departmental orientations. One director says, "[The orientation provides] specific and concrete information about what to do to get adjusted, [it] sends a message to students about the importance of fitting in." Another says, "[I sponsor] an orientation meeting before classes start with only the incoming class. We tell them what it's like to be in the department, what to do if they need help. We try to make it as clear as possible what is expected of them."

These smaller orientations serve a variety of purposes. They acquaint the students to the norms and requirements of that particular department. They also introduce the incoming graduate students to key members of the department, not only the faculty but also the support staff and the advanced graduate students. Finally, these orientations educate the students about the bureaucracy of the university and assist new students in negotiating the registration and financial aid processes.

Collegiality. Past research has linked collegiality with academic development. Students' interactions with other students in the graduate program are found to relate positively to academic achievement and career development (Blackwell, 1987; Hartnett, 1976). Environments that hinder peer interactions, such as competitive academic climates with an emphasis on grade achievement, were negatively related to scholarly socialization (Katz and Hartnett, 1976).

The identified best practices foster collegiality among the first-year students—for example, placing students in communal offices. If the incoming class is less than ten students, best practices dictate they all be assigned to the same office. If the incoming class is larger, groups of five to eight students can share several offices. These communal offices serve as places where students can informally socialize, have lunch together, and interact over homework problems and course requirements. Placing the students together in small groups fosters group interaction and aids the students' social integration into their new department—a task that has been speculated to be of greatest importance for the first year (Tinto, 1993). One graduate director identified their department's policy of assigning incoming students to communal offices as a way to help students feel like they are a part of the department, saying, "We do a good job [of making the students feel connected to the department] by putting the students together in courses and offices."

Collegiality is beneficial not only within but also between the graduate classes. The best practices identified here encourage interaction between first-year and advanced graduate students by assigning each incoming student to an advanced student. The advanced graduate students help new students navigate the bureaucratic process of registration, serve as informal advisors for course decisions, and provide emotional and social support for what may prove to be the most taxing year of graduate school. These relationships often extend past the early experiences and may evolve into informal mentoring roles that aid students in choosing advisors and deciding on research and writing projects. The students appreciate this assistance, especially with fulfilling aversive bureaucratic tasks.

The results of these efforts at collegiality seem to be paying off for the departments. The first-year students report feeling a part of the department and quickly identify a sense of camaraderie with their classmates. One says, "It is a large department but [there is] a lot of camaraderie among first years." Another says, "[I have been] impressed with the camaraderie among students, impressed how quickly these people, who have never known each other, become a family."

Mentoring. Mentoring may be the most important variable related to academic and career success for graduate students. Graduate research assistants who had intense professional interactions with supervisors evidenced greater research productivity compared with their peers (Malaney, 1988). Graduate students who reported having a number of faculty as "colleagues" and being treated like a "junior colleague" by one's advisor made better progress toward their degree (Berg and Ferber, 1983; Girves and Wemmerus, 1988). On the other hand, students who did not finish their dissertation list poor working relationships with their advisors or committee as one of the two most frequent reasons for terminating their graduate schooling; the other reason is financial difficulties (Jacks, Chubin, Porter, and Connolly, 1983).

Mentoring is most often thought important later in graduate school, when students are immersed in individual research and scholarship. The foundations for mentoring relationships, however, are being formed during the early years, when students are completing coursework. Consequently, the best departments in our study provided ample opportunities for students to get to know faculty in professional and social settings. The quality of mentoring relationships is not based solely on common research and scholarly interests but can be predicted on regularly scheduled, mutually beneficial professional interactions (Boyle and Boice, in press). We identified three best practices utilized by departments to foster mentorship.

First, assign incoming students to academic advisors. The role of these temporary advisors is to help students choose their courses during the first year of graduate education. This gives the students a definitive faculty contact with whom they can ask questions regarding courses. In most cases, students spend the majority of their time on coursework during the first year of graduate school (Boyle, 1996), so course-related, not research-related, counsel is most relevant.

Second, provide a structured protocol for students to obtain research advisors after the new graduate students have arrived on campus. Before this time, students may know about the research interests of the faculty, but rarely will students have any information about faculty's supervisory styles. By waiting to assign research advisors, future advisors and advisees can learn about each other in important ways that will greatly influence the quality of the mentoring.

One department provided a structured protocol to help students decide on research advisors. One first-year student describes it this way: "[I learned about my research advisor] because students initiate [interactions and] the department requires you to talk to [i.e., interview] at least three faculty to decide who to work with."

These interviews not only covered research interests but also provided opportunities for the faculty and students to determine whether their expectations and work habits were complementary. Faculty also sponsored open-house events where new students could talk with the advanced graduate students, thus providing opportunities for new students to learn how the advisors function as supervisors and mentors. The smaller departments could replace these open houses with events where advanced graduate students discuss their current research and scholarly activities, their advisors, and the methods of working with the advisors.

What does this accomplish for the students and the department? It allows students and faculty to get to know each other before committing to a long, close working relationship, and may prevent unsuccessful completion of degree requirements due to incompatible advising relationships (Jacks, Chubin, Porter, and Connolly, 1983).

Students given the opportunity to request research advisors after arrival on campus all identified common research interests and compatible working styles as important factors in choosing research advisors. Two first-year students described their reasons for choosing their advisor. The first student commented, "[I] like the research he's doing. [Plus I] like his personality, and he does care about students, will push you along, and help you get [research] skills." The second student said, "[I chose him] initially based on his research work, then from talking with graduate students who work with him. [I also] really like the other graduate students [in his laboratory]."

Third, provide opportunities for new students to socialize with all the faculty and advanced graduate students. The exemplary departments hosted significantly more social events than the lower-rated departments. These events were as frequent as weekly "happy hours." The faculty was well represented at these occasions, thus allowing the students and faculty to converse in an informal setting and become acquainted before the choices for research advisors and advisees had to be made. Students were also able to develop secondary mentoring relationships with faculty from whom they were not likely to take courses or work with on research or scholarly writing projects.

When these venues for fostering interaction between the first-year students and the faculty were in place, the students reported positive experiences in their initial adjustment period. One first-year student described it this way: "Professors deal with you, they are available to you, all the staff is more than helpful. Other graduate students from other years are pretty open to you, and professors genuinely are interested in having you look at their research groups."

Program Structure. When program structure was provided for graduate students—that is, short-term goals, structured assignments, and timely feedback—the graduate students completed degree requirements sooner and at higher rates than without such support (Dillon and Malott, 1981; Thomas, 1995). Because recent criticisms of graduate training have focused on the lack of structure that all too often occurs, some have suggested that graduate departments provide more structured training support and encourage regular meetings between faculty and students (Utley and Weitzman, 1993).

Program structure also promoted early involvement in scholarship in the exemplary departments. This structure was apparent almost immediately with the requirement that students attend research seminars. The research seminars might be weekly dinners hosted by faculty members for the first-year students, or pro-seminars where students listened to presentations by the faculty.

Exemplary departments provided short-term deadlines for getting students involved in research during the summer following the completion of their first year. Departmental procedures also ensured that the students received immediate feedback on their research efforts. How was this accomplished? After students were matched up with research advisors, they began their research and scholarly writing almost immediately. The department set a deadline for the fall semester of the student's second year for them to present the results of their scholarship. The deadline was well publicized and supported through precedent.

These forms of structure help create a culture in which students are clear about their duties. Consequently, students complete degree requirements more quickly, and both students and faculty benefit, achieving higher productivity in scholarship and research. One program director explained, "[Students have a requirement to work on] one paper intended to be based on research experience during the first year, [thus] pushing people to get some research experience early." An advanced graduate student states clearly, "The first summer is for research."

Overall, implementation of these best practices seems to foster an open and friendly environment within departments. The office doors of faculty within the exemplary departments were regularly open. The students felt free to meet with their academic and research advisors often. If the faculty members were unable to meet at a particular moment, they scheduled meetings for later times.

Not only did the exemplary departments have higher ratings for training graduate students, they also had higher ratings in terms of faculty scholarship (NRC, 1995). How can these faculty have time for students and still be productive scholars? First, regardless of whether from the humanities, social sciences, or physical/life sciences, faculty thoughtfully planned how to arrange research and scholarship projects to incorporate their graduate students. Even faculty in fields traditionally committed to individual, independent scholarship have made successful efforts to expand their scholarly activities to include their graduate students.

Second, the environments of collegiality, mentoring, and structure that these faculty have developed nurture the faculty as well (Boice, 1993). They, too, have been mentored, first as graduate students and later as new faculty. As they rise through the ranks of academia, they take on the role first of protégé, then of mentor. These faculty have developed their own supportive networks, having made networking a professional priority.

Finally, exemplary faculty make use of personal structure to sustain their own scholarly productivity, such as graphing their writing times and monitoring scholarship outputs. The departments with the best practices for enculturating graduate students have faculty who engage in similar best practices to support their own career advancement and satisfaction.

Conclusion

Graduate education is under scrutiny, much of which focuses on the high rates of attrition (Bowen and Rudenstine, 1992; Marcus, 1997). Addressing the high attrition rates requires evaluation of the early years of graduate education. In other fields, the early years have been identified as crucial for persistence and career advancement. The best practices we identified—collegiality, mentoring, and structure—help incoming graduate students adjust more readily to the culture and academic demands of the graduate department. These best practices also foster mutually beneficial professional relationships and early involvement in scholarship.

Best practices have been widely used in the fields of organizational and human resource development to achieve organizational excellence. Focusing on the experiences of employees within an organization benefits not only its members, but the organization as well. Organizations that offer training and career development for its members are rewarded with high productivity and organizational growth (London, 1995). Although a universal set of best practices does not exist (Capelli and Crocker-Hefter, 1996), all best practices are based on a belief or enduring commitment (Fitz-enz, 1997). The success of the departments we have discussed demonstrates that by striving for a culture in which collegiality and mentoring flourish from a basis of program structure, each department can develop its own version of best practices in graduate education.

References

Berg, H. M., and Ferber, M. A. "Men and Women Graduate Students: Who Succeeds and Why?" *Journal of Higher Education,* 1983, *54,* 629–648.

Blackwell, J. E. *Mainstreaming Outsiders: The Production of Black Professionals.* New York: General Hall, 1987.

Boice, R. "New Faculty Involvement for Women and Minorities." *Research in Higher Education,* 1993, *34,* 291–341.

Bowen, W. G., and Rudenstine, N. L. *In Pursuit of the Ph.D.* Princeton, N.J.: Princeton University Press, 1992.

Boyle, P. "Socialization Experiences of New Graduate Students." Unpublished doctoral dissertation, Department of Psychology, State University of New York at Stony Brook, 1996.

Boyle, P., and Boice, R. "Systematic Mentoring for New Faculty Teachers and Graduate Teaching Assistants." *Innovative Higher Education,* in press.

Clark, B. R. *Places of Inquiry: Research and Advanced Education in Modern Universities.* Berkeley: University of California Press, 1995.

Corcoran, M., and Clark, S. M. "Professional Socialization and Contemporary Career Attitudes of Three Faculty Generations." *Research in Higher Education,* 1984, *20,* 131–153.

Dillon, M. J., and Malott, R. W. "Supervising Masters Theses and Doctoral Dissertations." *Teaching of Psychology*, 1981, *8*, 195–202.

Fitz-enz, J. "The Truth About Best Practices: What They Are and How to Apply Them." *Human Resource Management*, 1997, *36*, 97–103.

Girves, G. E., and Wemmerus, V. "Developing Models of Graduate Student Degree Progress." *Journal of Higher Education*, 1988, *59*, 163–189.

Hartnett, R. T. "Environments for Advanced Learning." In J. Katz and R. T. Hartnett (eds.), *Scholars in the Making*. Cambridge, Mass.: Ballinger, 1976.

Jacks, P., Chubin, D. E., Porter, A. L., and Connolly, T. "The ABCs of ABDs: A Study of Incomplete Doctorates." *Improving College and University Teaching*, 1983, 32(2), 74–81.

Katz, J., and Hartnett, R. T. *Scholars in the Making*. Cambridge, Mass.: Ballinger, 1976.

London, M. (ed.). *Employees, Careers, and Job Creation: Developing Growth-Oriented Human Resource Strategies and Programs*. San Francisco: Jossey-Bass, 1995.

Malaney, G. D. "Graduate Education as an Area of Research in the Field of Higher Education." In J. C. Smart (ed.), *Higher Education: Handbook of Theory and Research*. Vol. 4. New York: Agathon Press, 1988.

Marcus, M. B. "Half a Doctor." *U.S. News and World Report*, April 7, 1997, p. 72.

National Research Council. *Research-Doctorate Programs in the United States: Continuity and Change*. Washington, D.C.: National Academy Press, 1995.

Thomas, C. "Helping Students Complete Masters Theses Through Active Supervision." *Journal of Management Education*, 1995, *19*(2), 240–249.

Tinto, V. *Leaving College: Rethinking the Causes and Cures of Student Attrition*. (2nd ed.) Chicago: University of Chicago Press, 1993.

Utley, A., and Weitzman, D. "Postgrad Provision Is Patchy, Ph.D. Practices Challenged for the First Time." *Times Higher Education Supplement*, July 30, 1993, p. iv.

Van Maanen, J., and Schein, E. "Toward a Theory of Organizational Socialization." *Research in Organizational Behavior*, 1979, *1*, 209–264.

PEG BOYLE is the mentoring specialist at MentorNet, a national electronic mentoring program that links female undergraduate and graduate science, engineering, and mathematics students with industry mentors.

BOB BOICE is retired and currently resides in Boone, North Carolina.

Graduate education is preparation, and it is a changing world for which graduate students must now prepare.

If We Want Things to Stay as They Are, Things Will Have to Change

Jules B. LaPidus

In 1960 Giuseppi di Lampedusa, the descendant of a noble family from Sicily, published his book *The Leopard* (di Lampedusa, English edition, 1960). The major character is the Prince, a powerful and thoughtful man growing old in a rapidly changing world. In a famous passage, the Prince's young nephew, Tancredi, who knows the world is changing and intends to be part of it, announces that he is going up into the mountains to fight with the rebels. When the Prince expresses surprise at this unusual action, Tancredi, in what is probably the book's best-known line, replies, "If we want things to stay as they are, then things will have to change." When I read the line, I thought it captured the mood of many current discussions about the future of universities and, particularly, about graduate education.

Today, roughly 85 percent of all master's degrees are practice-oriented, and the majority of master's students work and pursue their degree on a part-time basis. One of the consequences is that access to the courses and programs students want or need has become a major issue, and for the working, place-bound, student, often with family responsibilities, the opportunities signified by the terms *distance education* and *asynchronous learning* are among the wonders of the modern world.

For the student contemplating doctoral education, the issues are somewhat different. The time it takes is longer, and the rewards may be less certain.

This chapter was presented at the Sixth National Conference on the Education and Employment of Graduate Teaching Assistants held in Minneapolis, Minnesota, on November 8, 1997. Much of the section dealing with doctoral education was modified from LaPidus (1997).

For many years, the principal reason to undertake doctoral study was an intense interest in scholarly research and the desire to spend a life studying, writing, and teaching. Today, about half of the Ph.D.s seek jobs outside the academy, and those who do pursue academic positions find a new and rapidly changing set of conditions and values defining the enterprise. The number of part-time faculty is growing, as is the number of nonuniversity, for-profit, organizations in the education business. Surely there will continue to be a need for scholars to enlarge the knowledge base and to address the multitude of problems we face. There also will continue to be a need for teachers, but whether the teacher-scholar model survives or is supplanted by new and different ways of structuring learning, teaching, research, and universities remains to be seen. Things will change, and there is growing interest in how doctoral education can best prepare people for the future.

The ability to carry out an independent research project successfully has long been considered the primary and perhaps the sole criterion for obtaining a Ph.D. With few exceptions, however, employers of Ph.D.s claim that this is not the only thing they are looking for, and that opportunities to function as an independent investigator are increasingly limited. Though academia and industry are still attracted to candidates with outstanding research credentials, and prospective employers still ask candidates to present research seminars describing their dissertation projects, they are beginning to ask for more.

Increasingly, candidates for academic employment are being asked about their teaching experience and about their views on education, and some institutions (particularly liberal arts colleges or community colleges) may ask candidates to present a lecture rather than give a research seminar. Likewise, industrial employers may try to elicit a broader view of a candidates' research training, particularly as it relates to the interests of the company, than can be expressed by just examining the dissertation topic. These expectations of potential employers translate rather quickly into interest in a broader approach to graduate education.

Students and graduate faculty members alike are trying to understand the role of graduate education in

- Preparation for research
- Preparation for scholarship
- Preparation for faculty positions
- Preparation for industrial positions
- Preparation for other positions
- Preparation for life

My purpose here is to describe what is meant in each case and then to discuss briefly a variety of approaches currently in place or being considered by universities in the United States and several other countries.

Preparation for Research

American graduate schools are very good at preparing students for research, clearly among the best, if not the best in the world. There is not always agreement about motives or context. Is the product the research result or the researcher? Are the graduate students there to help the faculty with their research, or is it the other way around? The answer, at least in the United States, is yes to all of the above. We have prided ourselves on the ability to produce research and researchers as part of the same process. To do that, we have developed a system that involves coursework coupled with doing research under the supervision of an established researcher. Until recently, this has been a uniquely American idea. Students truly are prepared to do research in their area of specialization. They are required to demonstrate that they know the literature and the techniques and, furthermore, that they understand how to solve problems in their field. Several other countries are adopting or adapting this approach and developing coursework components in what were formerly research-only programs.

But the research experience has to extend beyond mere technical training. This has been expressed most clearly by John Ziman: "To be a member of a team directed by a distant and very busy leader, building just one technical link in a complicated experiment, is an adequate apprenticeship to the art; it is as if the pupils of Rubens were to be accounted artists after five years of painting-in the buttons on his larger compositions. High technical standards may be achieved by the student, without a grasp of the deeper intellectual issues" (Ziman, 1968).

Similarly, Ernest Boyer has observed, "Surely, scholarship means engaging in original research. But the work of the scholar also means stepping back from one's investigation, looking for connections, building bridges between theory and practice, and communicating one's knowledge effectively to students" (Boyer, 1990).

The point here is that graduate education must be more than a simple apprenticeship and that research, in this context, must be more than a technical exercise for producing research results. It must be a vehicle for preparing scholars.

Preparation for Scholarship

Scientists often seem uncomfortable with the word *scholarship,* which usually is associated with the humanities and somehow does not seem as rigorous as research. There is relatively little use of the term in science programs perhaps because scientists may believe that the term *scientist* subsumes the term *scholar.* Realistically, most Ph.D.s probably are what has been described as "operationally creative," that is, they have solid training in research and are very good at doing work and solving problems in their field. Trying to make students more scholarly, more aware of the implications of their work and how it fits into a bigger and more complex pattern, is much more difficult than teaching them how to carry out a procedure and interpret the results. It usually is accomplished informally, through interactions with colleagues, through seminars, and, rarely, through specific programmatic activities. I have suggested elsewhere (LaPidus, 1996) that research and scholarship may be related in much the same way as information and knowledge, and that if research is what you do, scholarship is the way you think about it. It is this broader view, this placing of one's research not just in the context of the discipline but in a larger framework of intellectual work, that distinguishes good graduate education from advanced training programs.

Preparation for Jobs and Careers

In considering preparation for jobs and/or careers, the component usually left out in discussions of the topic is the responsibility of the employer. Many, if not most, employers understand that graduate education does not produce completely formed professionals, ready to make a full contribution from the first day on the job. Good graduate programs produce people who are *prepared to become* faculty members or industrial researchers or practicing professionals in a host of fields. They have acquired knowledge and skills that make them well suited for a variety of different positions, but they may need to be assisted in adapting to those positions.

Preparation for Faculty Positions. Usually this is stated as preparation for teaching, but that is far too restricted a view of the faculty role. Faculty members do a lot more than teach. The new faculty member faces a daunting number of responsibilities. Those listed here represent the range of activities routinely carried out by faculty members at various times during their academic career:

- Developing and teaching graduate courses
- Doing research
- Getting financial support for research
- Writing and publishing books and/or articles in the scholarly literature
- Directing graduate student research
- Getting financial support of graduate students
- Advising and mentoring graduate students
- Developing and teaching courses in professional programs
- Developing and teaching undergraduate courses
- Writing textbooks and computer programs
- Advising and mentoring undergraduates
- Participating in academic, administrative and service responsibilities
- Bringing scholarship (that is, the ability to identify the important questions and suggest ways to find answers) to bear on all of the above

Historically there has been little, if any, "preparation" for any of these activities except research. In fact, for the most part, they are not even discussed. Being a teaching assistant (TA) provides some exposure to teaching, but the TA experience is often confined to lower-level courses and, in any case, usually is not thought of in terms of faculty preparation. During the past ten years, universities have been paying much more attention to the education and training of TAs, and the biannual conferences on the Education and Employment of Graduate Teaching Assistants have attracted hundreds of faculty members, administrators, and graduate students. But being a teaching assistant is only part of the preparation for faculty roles.

As an approach to improving this situation, a number of universities have developed programs to introduce graduate students to the full range of faculty life. The Preparing Future Faculty (PFF) program, administered by the Council of Graduate Schools and Association of American Colleges and Universities with funding from The Pew Charitable Trusts, is perhaps the most extensive of these. Fifteen clusters have been formed, each comprising a research university and a diverse group of institutions such as a comprehensive university, a four-year liberal arts college, and a community college, all situated so that students can move easily among them. Doctoral students participate, on a discipline basis, in faculty activities in all four types of institutions. This program deals with the realities of being a faculty member in the variety of settings that constitute the academic job market. Variations of this kind of program exist at dozens of universities.

Ellie Noam, in an article titled, "Electronics and the Dim Future of Universities," observed, "True teaching and learning are about more than information and its transmission. Education is based on mentoring, internalization, identification, role modeling, guidance, socialization, interaction, and group activity. In these processes, physical proximity plays an important role. Thus, the strength of the future physical university lies less in pure information and more in college as a community; less in wholesale lecture, and more in individual tutor; less in Cyber-U, and more in Goodbye-Mr. Chips College" (Noam, 1995). Noam is talking about education as a labor-intensive, interactive process through which people are not just informed, but can become knowledgeable.

We do not know what the expectation will be for faculty in the coming years. What is absolutely certain is that faculty will do many things in ways very different from those in the past. In situations like that, the general aspects of their preparation will change least rapidly with time and will provide a framework capable of supporting a variety of structures.

Preparation for Industrial Careers. This has been much less structured than preparation for faculty careers, and obviously applies primarily to the sciences and engineering. A number of institutions, in collaboration with industrial partners, have developed internships for doctoral and, in some cases, postdoctoral candidates. In 1974, the Teaching Company Scheme was initiated in Great Britain. This has mainly involved engineering students but has been expanding to include other fields. The term *teaching company* is analogous to *teaching hospital,* that is, a place where students can experience the research issues, as well as the culture, characteristic of a particular kind of setting. This may be a useful model to explore.

It is not unusual for science and engineering departments to develop industrial advisory groups. These involve researchers and research administrators from companies with interests in the research being carried out in the department and in the students being trained. They may meet on a regular basis with faculty and graduate students to discuss mutual research interests and to cultivate graduate students who may be future employees. These advisory groups provide some exposure to industrial research problems but little to industrial research culture. Combined with industrial internships, they may be of real value to graduate students interested in industrial careers. For example, the University of Wisconsin–Madison, has developed a biotechnology training program that involves a six-month industrial internship for graduate students.

Preparation for Other Jobs. We know that people with graduate degrees find their way into a variety of jobs and careers, some by choice, some by chance, and some by default. The further away from their specific training, the greater the use of their general education, particularly the scholarly process. John Armstrong, in a perceptive article titled "Rethinking the Ph.D.," stated what I believe to be the essence of the issue: "The training of new Ph.D.s is too narrow, too campus-centered, and too long. Furthermore, many new Ph.D.s have much too narrow a set of personal and career expectations. Most do not know what it is they know that is of most value. They think that what they know is how to solve certain highly technical and specialized problems. . . . Of course, what they really know is how to formulate questions and partially answer them, starting from powerful and fundamental points of view" (Armstrong, 1994).

The question then is: How do students discover "what they really know?" It may be that graduate educators have to become more explicit about it, rather than to hope it occurs by chance.

Preparation for Life

How far can or should graduate programs go in preparing students for life? Beyond ensuring that they know and can function competently in their field, have some broader concept of scholarship that extends beyond those fields, and recognize the ethical responsibilities inherent in research and teaching, what else can graduate schools do that makes sense and helps students? A number of reasonable suggestions have been made, most of which come down to providing better information about jobs, careers, options, and safety nets. At some point, each program, through open and realistic discussions involving students faculty, potential employers, and alumni, will have to develop ideas about what will provide the best graduate education.

Approaches to Change in Graduate Education

Several qualitatively different approaches are being suggested for improving the education of graduate students. Generally speaking, these approaches fall into several well-defined categories:

- Universities are trying to provide better information about jobs and the job market. Given the uncertainties in predicting or projecting what the job market will be when current students graduate, they need to be made aware that there are no guarantees, and that their graduate education is applicable to a variety of career options. Career services and career development offices usually have been geared to the needs of undergraduate students. Some universities have developed specialized services of this type for graduate students.

- Seminars or workshops on the relationship of graduate education to particular fields, and on how graduate education relates to work, are being offered or developed at some universities. Former graduates or other individuals involved in academic and nonacademic careers may talk about their career and the role graduate education played in their life. The University of Manchester Institute of Technology initiated the Graduate Support Program (Grasp) in 1994. First-year Ph.D. students are exposed to lectures on topics such as project planning, time management, report writing, ethics, presentation skills, communication skills, leadership and teamwork, stress management, and product design and development. Final-year doctoral students attend classes on job-hunting skills, curriculum vitae writing, job interviews, and industrial structures and organization.

- A number of universities are considering program modifications that will add more academic content. Here, several approaches prevail:

Develop minor or collections of courses (or certificates) in closely related areas—for example, molecular biology for organic chemists, economics for political scientists, computer science for physicists. The idea is to broaden the scope but stay close to the student's major field of study. The student would still plan to work in the primary area of interest but would have "added on" related skills.

Develop area studies options (perhaps as certificate programs) in very broad but related areas—for example, environmental studies, or medieval studies, or polar studies. In the social sciences, students have been doing this for years. For example, economists with special interests in Asia might take a certificate program in East Asian studies. The idea is to retain your expertise but relate it to a certain context or area of interest.

Develop courses, master's degrees, or certificate programs in presumably unrelated areas—for example, business, journalism, public health, education. In this case, the student is developing options that utilize the primary area as it applies to something else—sales, writing, K–12 teaching, and so on.

Develop programs similar to the Mres (Master of Research) degree recently initiated in the United Kingdom. Students from different disciplines are brought together to discuss and dissect research in a number of fields. The point is to illustrate the process of defining relevant questions and finding answers that is the basis for scholarly research in all fields. This kind of approach also emphasizes multidisciplinary aspects of problem solving. It is particularly useful for new graduate students.

Conclusion

Any or all of these suggestions may be appropriate for specific programs, departments, or universities. Some have been in place for years, some are now being considered, and some have recently been instituted. All suffer from the same drawback—they take time and increase the workload for students and faculty alike. Many people believe that such changes will increase the time it takes for students to earn their degree. Actually, the most important variables related to that issue are probably adequate financial support, realistic dissertation requirements, and effective mentoring. Compared with these variables, the program modifications suggested here will have relatively little effect on time to degree, and may lead to increased completion rates as well as improved quality of graduate education and career prospects of students.

We have come a long way from the one student, one professor, one research project concept of doctoral education and are beginning to understand that doctoral study is an educational experience designed to prepare students for a variety of roles and responsibilities, all centered on the applications of scholarship. This means more than simply adding on components; it requires examination of the basic purpose and goals of doctoral education. We need to decide which things we want to stay the same, and which things must change if we are to achieve a broader and more realistic view of graduate education—one that is consistent not only with the size and scope of the current enterprise but with the changing nature of education, work, society, and scholarship as we prepare to enter the twenty-first century.

References

Armstrong, J. "Rethinking the Ph.D." *Issues in Science and Technology,* Summer 1994, pp. 19–22.

Boyer, E. L. *Scholarship Reconsidered: Priorities of the Professoriate.* Princeton, N.J.: Carnegie Foundation for the Advancement of Teaching, 1990.

di Lampedusa, G. *The Leopard.* New York: Time-Life Books, 1960. (Reprinted 1966.)

LaPidus, J. B. "Scholarship and Research: Gresham's Law Revisited." *CGS Communicator,* 1996, 29(1).

LaPidus, J. B. "Doctoral Education: Preparation for the Future." *CGS Communicator,* 1997, 30(10).

Noam, E. M. "Electronics and the Dim Future of the University." *Science, 270,* 1995, 247–249.

Ziman, J. M. *Public Knowledge: An Essay Concerning the Social Dimension of Science.* Cambridge, England: Cambridge University Press, 1968.

JULES B. LAPIDUS received a doctorate in medicinal chemistry from the University of Wisconsin. He was a faculty member at The Ohio State University for twenty-six years, during the last ten of which he served as vice provost for research and dean of the graduate school. In 1984 he accepted his current position as president of the Council of Graduate Schools.

INDEX

Ordering Information

NEW DIRECTIONS FOR HIGHER EDUCATION is a series of paperback books that provides timely information and authoritative advice about major issues and administrative problems confronting every institution. Books in the series are published quarterly in Spring, Summer, Fall, and Winter and are available for purchase by subscription and individually.

SUBSCRIPTIONS cost $54.00 for individuals (a savings of 35 percent over single-copy prices) and $90.00 for institutions, agencies, and libraries. Standing orders are accepted. New York residents, add local tax for subscriptions. (For subscriptions outside the United States, add $7.00 for shipping via surface mail or $25.00 for air mail. Orders *must be prepaid* in U.S. dollars by check drawn on a U.S. bank or charged to VISA, MasterCard, or American Express.)

SINGLE COPIES cost $22.00 plus shipping (see below) when payment accompanies order. California, New Jersey, New York, and Washington, D.C., residents, please include appropriate sales tax. Canadian residents, add GST and any local taxes. Billed orders will be charged shipping and handling. No billed shipments to post office boxes. (Orders from outside the United States *must be prepaid* in U.S. dollars by check drawn on a U.S. bank or charged to VISA, MasterCard, or American Express.)

SHIPPING (SINGLE COPIES ONLY): $30.00 and under, add $5.50; to $50.00, add $6.50; to $75.00, add $7.50; to $100.00, add $9.00; to $150.00, add $10.00.

ALL PRICES are subject to change.

DISCOUNTS FOR QUANTITY ORDERS are available. Please write to the address below for information.

ALL ORDERS must include either the name of an individual or an official purchase order number. Please submit your order as follows:
    Subscriptions: specify series and year subscription is to begin
    Single copies: include individual title code (such as HE82)

MAIL ALL ORDERS TO:
    Jossey-Bass Publishers
    350 Sansome Street
    San Francisco, California 94104-1342

PHONE subscription or single-copy orders toll-free at (888) 378-2537 or at (415) 433-1767 (toll call).

FAX orders toll-free to: (800) 605-2665.

FOR SUBSCRIPTION SALES OUTSIDE OF THE UNITED STATES, contact any international subscription agency or Jossey-Bass directly.